Everyday
Mathematics®

Student Reference Book

The University of Chicago
School Mathematics Project

Everyday Mathematics®

Student Reference Book

The University of Chicago
School Mathematics Project

Mc Graw Hill **Wright Group**

The *McGraw·Hill* Companies

UCSMP Elementary Materials Component
Max Bell, Director

Authors
Max Bell, Jean Bell, John Bretzlauf, Amy Dillard, Robert Hartfield, Andy Isaacs, James McBride (Director), Kathleen Pitvorec, Peter Saecker

Technical Art
Diana Barrie

Research
Deborah Arron Leslie

Photo Credits
Phil Martin/Photography
Jack Demuth/Photography
Cover: Bill Burlingham/Photography
Photo Collage: Herman Adler Design

Permissions
page 84, Boys running: Peter Cade/Tony Stone Images
page 91, Railroad tracks: John Edwards/Tony Stone Images
page 181, Spider's web with dewdrops at sunrise: Hans Strand/Tony Stone Images
page 257, Tornado: Charles Doswell/Tony Stone Images
page 259, Nurse measures a child: Kevin Tanaka/*Chicago Tribune*

 **Wright Group**

Send all inquiries to:
Wright Group/McGraw-Hill
P.O. Box 812960
Chicago, IL 60681

Printed in the United States of America.

ISBN 0-07-584485-0

3 4 5 6 7 8 9 10 11 RRC 09 08 07 06 05 04

Contents

Numbers and Counting 1

Number Uses	2
Number Grids	6
Number Lines	10
Comparing Numbers	13
Name-Collection Boxes	14
Parentheses	16
Place Value for Counting Numbers	18
Using Fractions to Name Part of a Whole	22
Using Fractions to Name Part of a Collection	24
Using Fractions in Measuring	25
Other Uses of Fractions	26
Equivalent Fractions	27
Table of Equivalent Fractions	30
Comparing Fractions to $\frac{1}{2}$, 0, and 1	31
Decimals	33
Place Value for Decimals	35
Comparing Decimals	36
Factors of a Number and Prime Numbers	37
Even and Odd Numbers	38
Negative Numbers	39
Very Large and Very Small Numbers	41

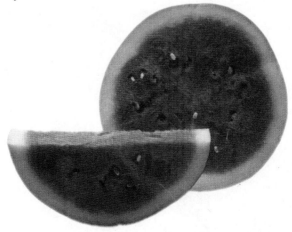

Operations and Computation 43

Basic Facts for Addition and Subtraction   44
Basic Facts for Multiplication and Division   46
Fact Triangles and Fact Families   48
Shortcuts   50
Partial-Sums Addition Method   51
Column Addition Method   53
Trade-First Subtraction Method   54
Left-to-Right Subtraction Method   56
Counting-Up Subtraction Method   57
Partial-Products Multiplication Method   58
Lattice Multiplication Method   60
Arrays   63
Multiplication and Equal Groups   65
Division and Equal Sharing   67
Division and Equal Grouping   68

Data and Chance 69

Tally Charts   70
Tally Charts and Line Plots   71
Describing a Set of Data: The Minimum, Maximum, and Range   73
Describing a Set of Data: The Median   74
Describing a Set of Data: The Mode   75
The Mean (Average)   77
Bar Graphs   80
Line Graphs   82
Chance and Probability   84

Geometry 87

Points and Line Segments   **88**
Rays and Lines   **89**
Angles   **90**
Parallel Lines and Segments   **91**
Line Segments, Rays, Lines, and Angles   **92**
Polygons   **94**
Triangles   **96**
Quadrangles   **98**
Circles   **100**
Geometric Solids   **102**
Polyhedrons   **104**
Pyramids   **105**
Prisms   **106**
Cylinders and Cones   **107**
Spheres   **108**
Congruent Figures   **109**
Line Symmetry   **111**

Measurement 113

Measurement Before the Invention of Standard Units   **114**
The Metric System   **116**
Measuring Length in Centimeters and Millimeters   **119**
Changing Units of Length in the Metric System   **122**
Personal References for Metric Units of Length   **123**
Measuring Length in Inches   **125**
Changing Units of Length in the U.S. Customary System   **128**
Personal References for U.S. Units of Length   **130**
Perimeter   **132**
Circumference and Diameter   **134**
Area   **136**
Volume   **139**
Capacity   **142**
Weight   **144**
Samples of Scales   **147**
Measuring Angles   **149**

Reference Frames   151

Temperature   **152**
Time   **156**
Calendars   **158**
Seasons and Length of Day   **160**
Coordinate Grids   **162**
Scale Drawings   **164**

Estimation   165

When You Have to Estimate   **166**
Ballpark Estimates   **167**
Estimate to Check Calculations   **168**
Adjusting Numbers   **169**

Patterns and Functions   171

Picture Patterns   **172**
Number Patterns   **174**
Frames and Arrows   **176**
Function Machines   **178**
Function Machines and "What's My Rule?"   **179**

Problem Solving   181

Solving Number Stories   **182**
Change Number Stories   **186**
Parts-and-Total Number Stories   **188**
Comparison Number Stories   **190**
Diagrams for Equal-Groups Problems   **191**

Games 193

Addition Top-It	**194**
Angle Race	**195**
Array Bingo	**197**
Baseball Multiplication	**198**
Baseball Multiplication (Advanced Version)	**200**
Beat the Calculator (Addition)	**202**
Beat the Calculator (Multiplication)	**203**
The Block-Drawing Game	**204**
Broken Calculator	**206**
Division Arrays	**207**
Equivalent Fractions Game	**208**
Equivalent Fractions Game (Advanced Version)	**209**
Factor Bingo	**210**
Fraction Top-It	**212**
Fraction Top-It (Advanced Version)	**213**
Less Than You!	**214**
Memory Addition/Subtraction	**215**
Missing Terms	**217**
Multiplication Bingo (Easy Facts)	**218**
Multiplication Bingo (All Facts)	**220**
Multiplication Draw	**221**
Multiplication Top-It	**222**
Name That Number	**224**
Number Top-It (5-Digit Numbers)	**226**
Number Top-It (7-Digit Numbers)	**228**
Number Top-It (3-Place Decimals)	**229**
Pick-a-Coin	**230**
Spinning to Win	**231**
Subtraction Top-It	**232**
Three Addends	**234**

Drinks Vending Machine Poster	**236**
Vending Machine Poster	**237**
Stationery Store Poster	**238**
Variety Store Poster	**239**
Stock-Up Sale Poster #1	**240**
Stock-Up Sale Poster #2	**241**
Animal Clutches	**242**
Normal Spring High and Low Temperatures (in °F)	**244**
September Rainfall	**245**
Shipping Packages: Rate Table	**246**
Shipping Packages: Zone Map	**247**
U.S. Road Mileage Map	**248**
Major U.S. City Populations	**250**
Sizes of Sport Balls	**252**
Weights of Sport Balls	**253**
Physical Fitness Standards	**254**
Record High and Low Temperatures	**256**
Tornado Data	**257**
World Population Growth	**258**
Heights of 8-Year-Old Children	**259**
Head Size	**260**
Number of Words Children Know	**262**
Letter Frequencies	**263**
Heights and Depths	**264**
How Much Would You Weigh on the Moon?	**265**
Ages of U.S. Presidents	**266**
Railroad Timetable and Airline Schedule	**267**
More Information about North American Animals	**268**
Tables of Measures	**270**
Glossary	**272**
Answer Key	**292**
Index	**299**

About the *Student Reference Book*

A reference book is a book that is organized to help people find information quickly or easily or both. Some reference books that you may have used are dictionaries, encyclopedias, cookbooks, and even phone books.

You can use this *Student Reference Book* to look up and review topics in mathematics. It has the following sections:

- A Table of Contents that lists the sections and shows how the book is organized. Each section has the same color band across the top of the pages.

- Essays within each section, such as Number Lines, Negative Numbers, Trade-First Subtraction Method, Bar Graphs, Triangles, Perimeter, Calendars, Ballpark Estimates, Number Patterns, and Solving Number Stories.

- Directions on how to play some of the mathematical games you may have played before.

- A Data Bank with posters, maps, and other information.

- A Glossary of mathematical terms consisting of brief definitions of important words.

- An Answer Key for every Check Your Understanding problem in the book.

- An Index to help you locate information quickly.

Numbers & Counting

Number Uses

Most people use hundreds or thousands of numbers each day. There are numbers on clocks, calendars, car license plates, postage stamps, scales, and so on. These numbers are used in many different ways. The major ways for using numbers are listed below.

1. Numbers are used as **counts.** A count is a number that tells "how many" things there are.

6 eggs

325 pages

The **counting numbers** are the numbers used in counting: 1, 2, 3, 4, 5, and so on.

2. Numbers are used as **measures.**

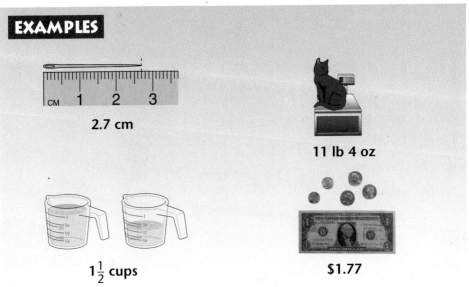

EXAMPLES

2.7 cm

11 lb 4 oz

$1\frac{1}{2}$ cups

$1.77

The numbers 1, 2, 3, and so on are the only numbers we use for counting. For measuring, we usually also use **decimal numbers** and **fractions.** For example, a ruler that shows only inch marks may not be useful for making accurate measurements. We need marks between the inch marks to show fractions of inches.

3. Numbers are used to show **locations** compared to some starting point.

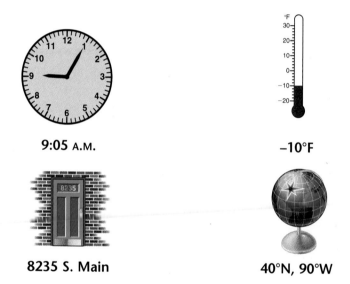

9:05 A.M.

−10°F

8235 S. Main

40°N, 90°W

Numbers in the street address 8235 S. Main give a location on Main Street. Clock times are locations in time, starting at noon or midnight. A pair of numbers like 40°N, 90°W gives a location on the Earth's surface compared to the location of the equator and the prime meridian.

three   3

Temperatures give a location on a thermometer starting at 0 degrees. We use negative numbers to show temperatures that are below 0 degrees. A temperature of $-10°F$ is read as "10 degrees below zero." The numbers -1, -2, -3, $-\frac{1}{2}$, and -31.6 are all negative numbers.

4. Numbers are used to make **comparisons.**

We often use numbers to compare two amounts or measures.

EXAMPLES

3 times as many boys as girls   The cat weighs $\frac{1}{2}$ **as much** as the dog.

5. Numbers are used as **codes.**

A code is a number used to identify some person or some thing. Codes are used in phone numbers, credit cards, and ZIP codes.

For example, in the ZIP code **60637:**

6 refers to the midwestern part of the United States

06 refers to Chicago

37 refers to a certain neighborhood in Chicago.

EXAMPLES

ISBN 1-57039-883-1

772-643-6608   M268-425-206

phone number   driver's license   bar code

Reminder: Most numbers come with a unit or symbol that tells what the number means: 10 cats, 10 inches, 10 A.M., and 10°F mean different things. The unit or symbol shows which meaning you want.

CHECK YOUR UNDERSTANDING

Decide whether each number is used to count, to measure, to show a location, to compare two quantities, or as a code.

1. 35 meters

2. 1-800-424-6000

3. 16 chickens

4. 10/15/99

5. 3 times as much

6. 1 lb 7 oz

7. 147 Poe St.

8. $4\frac{1}{2}$ inches

9. 254 children

10. $\frac{1}{2}$ as many

11. 12 noon

12. 12 minutes

13. 3:20 P.M.

14. 0 pink elephants

15. 100°C

16. 11:08 A.M.

Check your answers on page 292.

Number Grids

A monthly calendar is an example of a **number grid.** The numbers of the days of the month are listed in order.

The numbers are printed in boxes. The boxes are printed in rows. There are 7 boxes in each row because there are 7 days in a week.

JUNE

				1	2	3
4	5	6	7	8	9	10
11	12	13	14	15	16	17
18	19	20	21	22	23	24
25	26	27	28	29	30	

A number grid like the one you use in class is shown on the opposite page. The numbers are listed in order and printed in rows of boxes.

Counting forward on a number grid is like reading a calendar. When you reach the end of a line, you go to the next line and start at the left. Counting backward on a number grid is like reading a calendar backward.

−19	−18	−17	−16	−15	−14	−13	−12	−11	−10
−9	−8	−7	−6	−5	−4	−3	−2	−1	0
1	2	3	4	5	6	7	8	9	10
11	12	13	14	15	16	17	18	19	20
21	22	23	24	25	26	27	28	29	30
31	32	33	34	35	36	37	38	39	40
41	42	43	44	45	46	47	48	49	50
51	52	53	54	55	56	57	58	59	60
61	62	63	64	65	66	67	68	69	70
71	72	73	74	75	76	77	78	79	80
81	82	83	84	85	86	87	88	89	90
91	92	93	94	95	96	97	98	99	100
101	102	103	104	105	106	107	108	109	110
111	112	113	114	115	116	117	118	119	120

The numbers on a number grid have some simple patterns. These patterns make the grid easy to use.

When you move *right,* numbers *increase by 1.*
(16 is 1 more than 15)

When you move *left,* numbers *decrease by 1.*
(23 is 1 less than 24)

When you move *down,* numbers *increase by 10.*
(75 is 10 more than 65)

When you move *up,* numbers *decrease by 10.*
(91 is 10 less than 101)

seven **7**

EXAMPLE Part of a number grid is shown below.

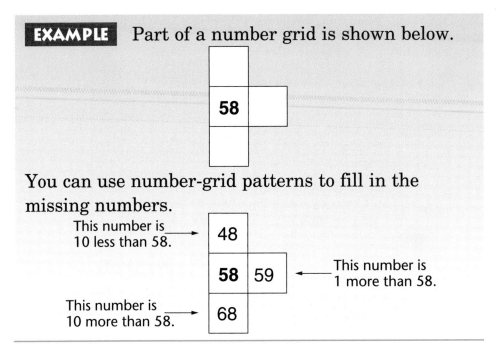

You can use number-grid patterns to fill in the missing numbers.

This number is 10 less than 58. → 48

58 59 ← This number is 1 more than 58.

This number is 10 more than 58. → 68

A number grid can help you find the difference between two numbers.

EXAMPLE Find the difference between 37 and 64.

31	32	33	34	35	36	(37)	38	39	40
41	42	43	44	45	46	47	48	49	50
51	52	53	54	55	56	57	58	59	(60)
61	62	63	64	65	66	67	68	69	70

- Start at 37.
- Count the number of *tens* going down to 57. There are 2 tens, or 20.
- Count the number of *ones* going right from 57 to 64. There are 7 ones, or 7.
- The difference between 37 and 64 is 2 tens and 7 ones, or 27.

Number grids can also be used to explore number patterns.

EXAMPLE Start with 0. Count by 2s until you reach 100.

									0
1	2	3	4	5	6	7	8	9	10
11	12	13	14	15	16	17	18	19	20
21	22	23	24	25	26	27	28	29	30
31	32	33	34	35	36	37	38	39	40
41	42	43	44	45	46	47	48	49	50
51	52	53	54	55	56	57	58	59	60
61	62	63	64	65	66	67	68	69	70
71	72	73	74	75	76	77	78	79	80
81	82	83	84	85	86	87	88	89	90
91	92	93	94	95	96	97	98	99	100

- The blue boxes contain *even* numbers.
- The yellow boxes contain *odd* numbers.

CHECK YOUR UNDERSTANDING

1. What is the difference between 28 and 63?

2. Copy the parts of the number grids shown. Use number-grid patterns to find the missing numbers.

a.

	98

b.

	316

Check your answers on page 292.

Number Lines

A **number line** is a line with numbers marked on it. An example is shown below.

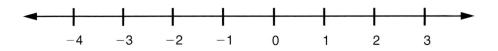

The number 0 is called the **zero point.** All of the spaces between marks are the same length.

The numbers to the right of 0 are called **positive numbers.** The numbers to the left of 0 are called **negative numbers.** For example, −3 is called "negative 3."

EXAMPLE The number line below shows the numbers −1, 0, 1, 2, and 3.

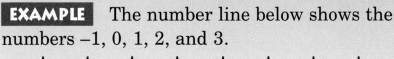

Marks have been drawn halfway between the numbered marks.
We can write in the numbers for these halfway marks.
The number line will look like this:

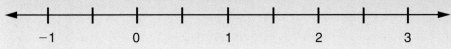

Every ruler is a number line. If the zero mark is at the end of the ruler, the number 0 may not be printed on the ruler.

On rulers, inches are usually divided into halves, quarters, eighths, and sixteenths. The marks to show fractions of an inch are usually of different sizes.

Every thermometer is a number line.

The zero mark on a Celsius scale (0°C) is the temperature at which water freezes.

Negative numbers are shown on the thermometer. A temperature of −16°C is read as "16 degrees below zero."

The marks on a thermometer are evenly spaced. The space between marks is usually 2 degrees.

Here is an easy method you can use to fill in the missing numbers on a number line:

1. Find the distance between the endpoints.

2. Count the spaces between the endpoints.

3. This fraction gives the length of each space.

$$\frac{\text{numerator is the distance}}{\text{denominator is the number of spaces}}$$

EXAMPLE Fill in the number line.

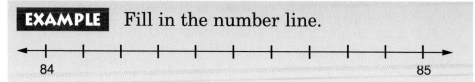

1. The distance from 84 to 85 is 1.
2. There are 10 spaces between 84 and 85.
3. Write the fraction $\frac{1}{10}$. The length of each space is $\frac{1}{10}$ or 0.1.

Here is the filled-in number line:

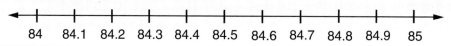

84 84.1 84.2 84.3 84.4 84.5 84.6 84.7 84.8 84.9 85

EXAMPLE Fill in the number line.

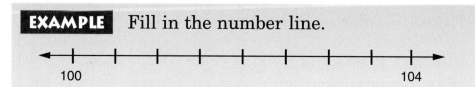

100   104

1. The distance from 100 to 104 is 4.
2. There are 8 spaces between 100 and 104.
3. Write the fraction $\frac{4}{8}$. $\frac{4}{8} = \frac{1}{2}$. The length of each space is $\frac{1}{2}$.

Here is the filled-in number line:

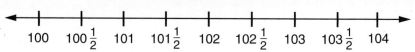

100 $100\frac{1}{2}$ 101 $101\frac{1}{2}$ 102 $102\frac{1}{2}$ 103 $103\frac{1}{2}$ 104

CHECK YOUR UNDERSTANDING
Copy the number line. Write the missing numbers.

50   52

Check your answers on page 292.

Comparing Numbers

When two numbers are **compared,** two results are possible:

- The numbers are **equal.**

- The numbers are **not equal.**
  One of the numbers is larger than the other.

Different symbols are used to show that numbers are equal or not equal.

- Use an **equal sign (=)** to show that the numbers are *equal*.

- Use a **greater-than symbol (>)** or a **less-than symbol (<)** to show that the numbers are *not equal*.

$$5 > 2 \quad 2 < 5$$

EXAMPLE	The table below lists other examples.

Symbol	Meaning	Examples
=	"equals" "is the same as"	$20 = 4 \times 5$ 3 cm = 30 mm $\frac{1}{2} = 0.5$
>	"is greater than"	14 ft 7 in. > 13 ft 11 in. $1.23 > 1.2$
<	"is less than"	$2\frac{1}{2} < 4$ 8 thousand < 12,000,000

Name-Collection Boxes

Any number can be written in many different ways. Different names for the same number are called **equivalent names.**

A **name-collection box** is a place to write names for the same number. It is a box with an open top and a label attached to it.

• The name on the label gives a number.

• The names written inside the box are equivalent names for the name on the label.

EXAMPLE   A name-collection box for 12 is shown below. It is called a "12-box."

12

3×4

1.2×10 twelve

$\frac{12}{1}$ *doce*

$3 + 3 + 3 + 3$

卌 卌 ||

$12 + 0$

• • •
• • •
• • •
• • •

To form equivalent names for numbers, you can

• add, subtract, multiply, or divide

• use tally marks or arrays

• write words in English or other languages

EXAMPLE A name-collection box for 100 is shown below. It is called a "100-box."

100

$200 \div 2$

1 more than 99

20×5

one hundred

$50 + 50$

Each name in the 100-box is a different way to say the number 100. This means that we can use an equal sign to write each statement below.

$$100 = 20 \times 5 \qquad 100 = 50 + 50$$

$$200 \div 2 = 100 \qquad \text{one hundred} = 100$$

CHECK YOUR UNDERSTANDING

What name belongs on the label for this name-collection box?

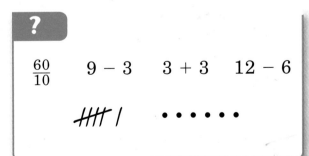

?

$\frac{60}{10}$ $9 - 3$ $3 + 3$ $12 - 6$

꜡꜡꜡ I   • • • • • •

Check your answer on page 292.

Parentheses

What does 15 − 3 + 2 equal? Should you *add* or *subtract* first?

We use **parentheses ( )** in number problems to tell which operation to do first.

EXAMPLE What does (15 − 3) + 2 equal?

The parentheses tell you to subtract first. 15 − 3 = 12.
Then add 12 + 2.

The answer is 14.

EXAMPLE What does 15 − (3 + 2) equal?

The parentheses tell you to add first. 3 + 2 = 5.
Then subtract 15 − 5.

The answer is 10.

EXAMPLE 5 × (9 − 2) = ?

The parentheses tell you to subtract 9 − 2 first.
9 − 2 = 7. Then multiply 5 × 7. This equals 35.

So 5 × (9 − 2) = 35.

EXAMPLE What does (2 × 3) + (4 × 5) equal?

There are 2 sets of parentheses. Solve each problem that is inside parentheses first. 2 × 3 = 6 and 4 × 5 = 20. Then add these answers. 6 + 20 = 26.

The answer is 26.

Sometimes a number statement does not have parentheses. You are asked to add parentheses.

EXAMPLE Make this number statement true by adding parentheses: $18 - 6 + 3 \times 4$

There are two ways to add parentheses:

$$18 = (6 + 3) \times 4$$

Add first. $6 + 3 = 9$
Then multiply. $9 \times 4 = 36$

18 is not equal to 36.
This statement is false.

and $18 = 6 + (3 \times 4)$

Multiply first. $3 \times 4 = 12$
Then add. $6 + 12 = 18$

18 is equal to 18.
This statement is true.

The correct way to add parentheses is
$18 = 6 + (3 \times 4)$.

CHECK YOUR UNDERSTANDING

1. Find the answer.

   a. $(4 \times 4) + 10 = ?$ **b.** $(60 - 40) \times 10 = ?$

   c. $? = (4 - 2) + (3 \times 3)$ **d.** $(8 - 4) \times 3 = ?$

2. Add parentheses to make each statement true.

   a. $20 - 8 + 3 = 15$ **b.** $20 = 5 + 3 \times 5$

   c. $3 \times 6 + 13 = 57$ **d.** $2 \times 3 + 1 \times 2 = 16$

Check your answers on page 292.

Place Value for Counting Numbers

People all over the world write numbers in the same way. This system of writing numbers was invented in India more than 1,000 years ago.

Any number can be written using the **digits** 0, 1, 2, 3, 4, 5, 6, 7, 8, and 9. The **place** that each digit has in a number is very important.

EXAMPLE The numbers 72 and 27 use the same digits, a 7 and a 2. But 72 and 27 are different numbers because the 7 and the 2 are in different places.

tens place	ones place		tens place	ones place
7	2		2	7

The digit 2 in 72 is worth 2.
The digit 2 in 27 is worth 20.

The digit 7 in 72 is worth 70.
The digit 7 in 27 is worth 7.

EXAMPLE The number 55 uses the digit 5 twice. But the two 5s are in different places.

tens place	ones place
5	5

The 5 in the tens place is worth 50.
The 5 in the ones place is worth 5.

We can use a **place-value chart** to show
how much each digit in a number is worth.
The **place** for a digit is its position in the number.
The **value** of a digit is how much it is worth.

EXAMPLE The number 25,513 is shown in the
place-value chart below.

10,000s	1,000s	100s	10s	1s
10 thousands place	thousands place	hundreds place	tens place	ones place
2	5	5	1	3

The digit 3 in the 1s place is worth $3 \times 1 = 3$.
The digit 1 in the 10s place is worth $1 \times 10 = 10$.
The digit 5 in the 100s place is worth $5 \times 100 = 500$.
The digit 5 in the 1000s place is worth $5 \times 1,000 = 5,000$.
The digit 2 in the 10,000s place is worth $2 \times 10,000 = 20,000$.
25,513 is read as "twenty-five thousand, five hundred thirteen."

For larger numbers we can use larger place-value
charts. The number 6,425,513 is shown in the
place-value chart below.

	Millions			**Thousands**			**Ones**	
hundred-millions	ten-millions	millions	hundred-thousands	ten-thousands	thousands	hundreds	tens	ones
6	4	2	5	5	1	3

A place-value chart can be used to compare two numbers.

EXAMPLE Compare the numbers 52,479 and 52,947. Which number is greater?

10,000s	1,000s	100s	10s	1s
10 thousands	thousands	hundreds	tens	ones
5	2	4	7	9
5	2	9	4	7

Start at the left side.

The 10,000s digits are the same. They are both worth 50,000.

The 1,000s digits are the same. They are both worth 2,000.

The 100s digits are *not* the same. The 4 is worth 400 and the 9 is worth 900.

So 52,947 is the larger number.

EXAMPLES Phil and Meg use place-value charts to write the number 35.

Phil	
10s	**1s**
3	5

Meg	
10s	**1s**
2	15

Phil's chart shows 3 tens and 5 ones. This is 30 + 5 = 35.

Meg's chart shows 2 tens and 15 ones. This is 20 + 15 = 35. Meg's way of filling in the place-value chart may be unusual, but it is correct.

Phil and Meg are both correct.

CHECK YOUR UNDERSTANDING

1. Count by 10s from 264. Write the next ten numbers.

2. Write the number that has
   8 in the tens place,
   6 in the 10 thousands place,
   7 in the ones place,
   0 in the hundreds place, and
   1 in the thousands place.

3. Write the number that is 1,000 more.
   a. 5,473   **b.** 9,870

4. Write the number that is 1,000 less.
   a. 4,561   **b.** 1,982

5. What is the largest 3-digit number you can make using the digits 4, 6, and 3?

Check your answers on page 292.

Using Fractions to Name Part of a Whole

The numbers $\frac{1}{2}$, $\frac{3}{4}$, $\frac{5}{4}$, and $\frac{25}{100}$ are all **fractions.** A fraction is written with two numbers. The top number of a fraction is called the **numerator.** The bottom number is called the **denominator.**

When naming fractions, we name the numerator first. Then we name the denominator.

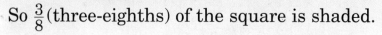

three-fourths $\frac{3}{4}$ ◄—— numerator ——► $\frac{25}{100}$ twenty-five hundredths
◄—— denominator ——►

Fractions can be useful when we want to name part of a whole object.

EXAMPLE   What fraction of this square is shaded?

The whole object is the square.

It has been divided into 8 equal parts.

Each part is $\frac{1}{8}$ (one-eighth) of the square.

Three of the parts are shaded.

So $\frac{3}{8}$ (three-eighths) of the square is shaded.

$\frac{3}{8}$ The *numerator* 3 tells the number of *shaded* parts.
The *denominator* 8 tells the number of equal parts in the *whole* square.

EXAMPLE What fraction of this circle is shaded?

The circle is divided into 12 equal parts.
Each part is $\frac{1}{12}$ (one-twelfth) of the circle.
Five of the parts are shaded.

The shaded part is $\frac{5}{12}$ (five-twelfths) of the circle.

When the numerator is zero, the fraction is equal to zero.

EXAMPLE

$\frac{0}{2}, \frac{0}{8}, \frac{0}{12}, \frac{0}{100}$ Each of these fractions equals 0.

When the numerator and denominator are the same, the fraction is equal to 1.

EXAMPLE

$\frac{2}{2}, \frac{7}{7}, \frac{8}{8}, \frac{100}{100}$ Each of these fractions equals 1.

CHECK YOUR UNDERSTANDING

1. Write each of these fractions.

   a. two-thirds b. three-sixteenths c. zero-thirds

2. What fraction names each shaded part?
   Write the fraction as a number and with words.

   a. b. c. d.

Check your answers on page 293.

Using Fractions to Name Part of a Collection

Fractions can be used to name part of a collection.

EXAMPLE What fraction of the buttons are small?

There are 7 buttons in all.

Three buttons are small.

Three out of 7 buttons are small.

This fraction shows what part of the button collection is small buttons:

$\frac{3}{7}$ ◄──── number of small buttons
number of buttons in all

$\frac{3}{7}$ (three-sevenths) of the buttons are small.

EXAMPLE What fraction of the dots are circled?

There are 12 dots.

Seven dots are circled.

Seven out of 12 dots are circled.

The fraction of dots circled is $\frac{7}{12}$.

Using Fractions in Measuring

Fractions can be used to make more careful measurements.

Think about the inch scale on a ruler. Suppose that the spaces between the whole inch marks are left unmarked. With a ruler like this, we can measure only to the nearest inch.

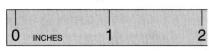

Ruler has inch marks only.
We can measure to nearest inch.

When we mark the spaces between inch marks, we can measure to the nearest $\frac{1}{2}$ inch and $\frac{1}{4}$ inch.

Ruler has $\frac{1}{4}$ and $\frac{1}{2}$ inch marks.
We can measure to nearest $\frac{1}{4}$ inch.

Other measuring tools are marked to show fractions of a unit. Measuring cups usually have $\frac{1}{4}$-cup, $\frac{1}{2}$-cup, and $\frac{3}{4}$-cup marks. Kitchen scales usually have ounce marks that divide the pound marks. 1 pound = 16 ounces. So 1 ounce equals $\frac{1}{16}$ pound.

Be careful. Always say or write the unit that you used in measuring. If you measured an object using an inch scale, then give the length in inches. If you weighed an object to the nearest pound, then give the weight in pounds.

Other Uses of Fractions

Fractions can name points on a number line that are "in between" the points that are already named.

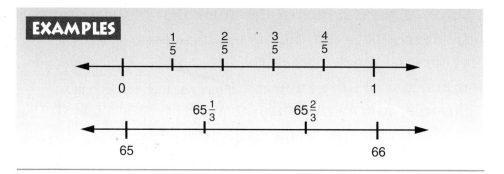

EXAMPLES

Fractions can be used to describe the chances that events will happen.

EXAMPLE This spinner has $\frac{1}{3}$ of the circle colored green. $\frac{2}{3}$ of the circle is not colored.

When we spin this spinner, there is a $\frac{1}{3}$ chance it will land on green.

If we spin it many times, it will land on green about $\frac{1}{3}$ of the time.

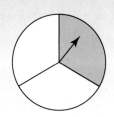

Fractions can be used to compare two numbers.

EXAMPLE Kay has $50. Faith has $25. Compare Faith's and Kay's amounts.

Faith has $\frac{1}{2}$ as much money as Kay.

Equivalent Fractions

Different fractions that name the same amount are called **equivalent fractions.**

Two circles are shown below. The top half of each circle is shaded. The circles are the same size. The first circle is divided into 2 equal parts. The second is divided into 6 equal parts.

  2 equal parts
1 part is shaded
$\frac{1}{2}$ circle is shaded

  6 equal parts
3 parts are shaded
$\frac{3}{6}$ circle is shaded

The shaded amounts are the same. So $\frac{3}{6}$ of the circle is the same as $\frac{1}{2}$ of the circle.

The fractions $\frac{3}{6}$ and $\frac{1}{2}$ are equivalent fractions.

We write $\frac{3}{6} = \frac{1}{2}$.

EXAMPLE Eight children go to a party. Two are girls. Six are boys.

 $\frac{1}{4}$ of the children are girls

 $\frac{2}{8}$ of the children are girls

$\frac{1}{4}$ of the children is the same as $\frac{2}{8}$ of the children. The fractions $\frac{1}{4}$ and $\frac{2}{8}$ are equivalent fractions.

We write $\frac{1}{4} = \frac{2}{8}$.

EXAMPLE A rectangle can be used to show fractions that are equivalent to $\frac{3}{4}$.

A rectangle is divided into quarters.
3 quarters are shaded.

So $\frac{3}{4}$ of the rectangle is shaded.

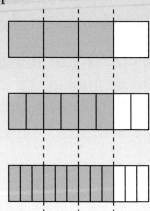

Each quarter is divided into 2 equal parts. There are 8 equal parts.
6 parts are shaded.

So $\frac{6}{8}$ of the rectangle is shaded.

Each quarter is divided into 3 equal parts. There are 12 equal parts.
9 parts are shaded.

So $\frac{9}{12}$ of the rectangle is shaded.

The fractions $\frac{3}{4}$, $\frac{6}{8}$, and $\frac{9}{12}$ all name the same shaded amount. They are all equivalent fractions.

EXAMPLE Equivalent fractions can be used to read the inch scale on a ruler.

$\frac{3}{4}$ or $\frac{6}{8}$ or $\frac{12}{16}$

The tip of the nail falls at the $\frac{3}{4}$-inch mark.

The length can be read as $\frac{3}{4}$ in. or $\frac{6}{8}$ in. or $\frac{12}{16}$ in.

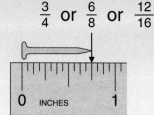

$\frac{3}{4}$, $\frac{6}{8}$, and $\frac{12}{16}$ all name the same mark on the ruler.

They are equivalent fractions.

There are two shortcut rules for finding **equivalent fractions**.

Method 1: Write the fraction.

Multiply both the numerator and the denominator by the same number.

EXAMPLE Find fractions that are equivalent to $\frac{1}{3}$.

$$\frac{1 \times 2}{3 \times 2} = \frac{2}{6} \qquad \frac{1 \times 4}{3 \times 4} = \frac{4}{12} \qquad \frac{1 \times 10}{3 \times 10} = \frac{10}{30}$$

$\frac{1}{3}, \frac{2}{6}, \frac{4}{12}$, and $\frac{10}{30}$ are all equivalent fractions.

Method 2: Write the fraction.

Divide both the numerator and the denominator by the same number.

EXAMPLE Find fractions that are equivalent to $\frac{12}{24}$.

$$\frac{12 \div 6}{24 \div 6} = \frac{2}{4} \qquad \frac{12 \div 4}{24 \div 4} = \frac{3}{6} \qquad \frac{12 \div 12}{24 \div 12} = \frac{1}{2}$$

$\frac{12}{24}, \frac{2}{4}, \frac{3}{6}$, and $\frac{1}{2}$ are all equivalent fractions.

CHECK YOUR UNDERSTANDING

1. Write 3 fractions that are equivalent to $\frac{1}{2}$.

2. Write 3 fractions that are equivalent to $\frac{40}{60}$.

Check your answers on page 293.

Table of Equivalent Fractions

The table below lists equivalent fractions. All of the fractions in a row name the same number.

Simplest Name	Equivalent Fraction Names								
0 (zero)	$\frac{0}{1}$	$\frac{0}{2}$	$\frac{0}{3}$	$\frac{0}{4}$	$\frac{0}{5}$	$\frac{0}{6}$	$\frac{0}{7}$	$\frac{0}{8}$	$\frac{0}{9}$
1 (one)	$\frac{1}{1}$	$\frac{2}{2}$	$\frac{3}{3}$	$\frac{4}{4}$	$\frac{5}{5}$	$\frac{6}{6}$	$\frac{7}{7}$	$\frac{8}{8}$	$\frac{9}{9}$
$\frac{1}{2}$	$\frac{2}{4}$	$\frac{3}{6}$	$\frac{4}{8}$	$\frac{5}{10}$	$\frac{6}{12}$	$\frac{7}{14}$	$\frac{8}{16}$	$\frac{9}{18}$	$\frac{10}{20}$
$\frac{1}{3}$	$\frac{2}{6}$	$\frac{3}{9}$	$\frac{4}{12}$	$\frac{5}{15}$	$\frac{6}{18}$	$\frac{7}{21}$	$\frac{8}{24}$	$\frac{9}{27}$	$\frac{10}{30}$
$\frac{2}{3}$	$\frac{4}{6}$	$\frac{6}{9}$	$\frac{8}{12}$	$\frac{10}{15}$	$\frac{12}{18}$	$\frac{14}{21}$	$\frac{16}{24}$	$\frac{18}{27}$	$\frac{20}{30}$
$\frac{1}{4}$	$\frac{2}{8}$	$\frac{3}{12}$	$\frac{4}{16}$	$\frac{5}{20}$	$\frac{6}{24}$	$\frac{7}{28}$	$\frac{8}{32}$	$\frac{9}{36}$	$\frac{10}{40}$
$\frac{3}{4}$	$\frac{6}{8}$	$\frac{9}{12}$	$\frac{12}{16}$	$\frac{15}{20}$	$\frac{18}{24}$	$\frac{21}{28}$	$\frac{24}{32}$	$\frac{27}{36}$	$\frac{30}{40}$
$\frac{1}{5}$	$\frac{2}{10}$	$\frac{3}{15}$	$\frac{4}{20}$	$\frac{5}{25}$	$\frac{6}{30}$	$\frac{7}{35}$	$\frac{8}{40}$	$\frac{9}{45}$	$\frac{10}{50}$
$\frac{2}{5}$	$\frac{4}{10}$	$\frac{6}{15}$	$\frac{8}{20}$	$\frac{10}{25}$	$\frac{12}{30}$	$\frac{14}{35}$	$\frac{16}{40}$	$\frac{18}{45}$	$\frac{20}{50}$
$\frac{3}{5}$	$\frac{6}{10}$	$\frac{9}{15}$	$\frac{12}{20}$	$\frac{15}{25}$	$\frac{18}{30}$	$\frac{21}{35}$	$\frac{24}{40}$	$\frac{27}{45}$	$\frac{30}{50}$
$\frac{4}{5}$	$\frac{8}{10}$	$\frac{12}{15}$	$\frac{16}{20}$	$\frac{20}{25}$	$\frac{24}{30}$	$\frac{28}{35}$	$\frac{32}{40}$	$\frac{36}{45}$	$\frac{40}{50}$
$\frac{1}{6}$	$\frac{2}{12}$	$\frac{3}{18}$	$\frac{4}{24}$	$\frac{5}{30}$	$\frac{6}{36}$	$\frac{7}{42}$	$\frac{8}{48}$	$\frac{9}{54}$	$\frac{10}{60}$
$\frac{5}{6}$	$\frac{10}{12}$	$\frac{15}{18}$	$\frac{20}{24}$	$\frac{25}{30}$	$\frac{30}{36}$	$\frac{35}{42}$	$\frac{40}{48}$	$\frac{45}{54}$	$\frac{50}{60}$

Comparing Fractions
to $\frac{1}{2}$, 0, and 1

Shading on the Fraction Cards makes it clear
whether a fraction is less than $\frac{1}{2}$, greater than $\frac{1}{2}$,
or equal to $\frac{1}{2}$.

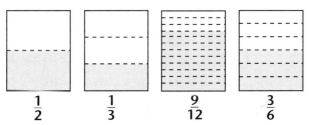

$$\frac{1}{2} \qquad \frac{1}{3} \qquad \frac{9}{12} \qquad \frac{3}{6}$$

You can also look at the numerator and denominator.

- If the numerator is less than half of the
  denominator, the fraction is less than $\frac{1}{2}$.
  For example, in $\frac{1}{3}$, 1 is less than half of 3.

- If the numerator is more than half of the ·
  denominator, the fraction is more than $\frac{1}{2}$.
  For example, in $\frac{9}{12}$, 9 is more than half of 12.

- If the numerator is exactly half of the
  denominator, the fraction is equal to $\frac{1}{2}$.
  For example, in $\frac{3}{6}$, 3 is half of 6.

You can use the greater-than symbol ($>$) or the
less-than symbol ($<$) when comparing fractions to $\frac{1}{2}$.

EXAMPLE $\frac{9}{12} > \frac{1}{2}$ means that $\frac{9}{12}$ is greater than $\frac{1}{2}$.

$\frac{1}{2} < \frac{9}{12}$ means that $\frac{1}{2}$ is less than $\frac{9}{12}$.

$\frac{4}{6} > \frac{1}{2}$ means that $\frac{4}{6}$ is greater than $\frac{1}{2}$.

Shading on the Fraction Cards also makes it clear whether a fraction is close to 0 or close to 1.

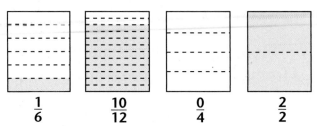

$$\frac{1}{6} \qquad \frac{10}{12} \qquad \frac{0}{4} \qquad \frac{2}{2}$$

You can also look at the numerator and denominator.

- If the numerator of the fraction is small compared to the denominator, the fraction is close to 0.
- If the numerator of the fraction is close to the denominator, the fraction is close to 1.

CHECK YOUR UNDERSTANDING

Compare each fraction to $\frac{1}{2}$. Use $<$, $>$, or $=$.

1. $\frac{5}{8} \square \frac{1}{2}$ **2.** $\frac{1}{2} \square \frac{7}{10}$ **3.** $\frac{2}{4} \square \frac{1}{2}$

4. $\frac{2}{10} \square \frac{1}{2}$ **5.** $\frac{1}{2} \square \frac{40}{80}$ **6.** $\frac{1}{3} \square \frac{1}{2}$

Use the Fraction Cards to help you.
Write *close to 1* or *close to 0.*

7. $\frac{3}{10}$ **8.** $\frac{7}{8}$ **9.** $\frac{2}{12}$

10. $\frac{1}{5}$ **11.** $\frac{0}{4}$ **12.** $\frac{48}{50}$

Check your answers on page 293.

Decimals

The numbers 0.3, 7.4, 0.46, and 23.456 are all **decimals.** Decimals are another way to write fractions.

Money amounts are decimals with a dollar sign in front of the number. In the amount $3.42, the 3 names whole dollars and the 42 names part of a dollar. The dot is called a **decimal point.**

Decimals have names. These names follow a simple pattern. The pattern for reading decimals is easy if you think of money. A dime is $\frac{1}{10}$ (one-tenth) of a dollar. A penny is $\frac{1}{100}$ (one-hundredth) of a dollar. Here are examples of the pattern:

Pattern for Tenths

Fraction Name	Read the Number	Decimal Name
$\frac{1}{10}$	1 tenth	0.1
$\frac{2}{10}$	2 tenths	0.2
$\frac{5}{10}$	5 tenths	0.5
$\frac{8}{10}$	8 tenths	0.8

Pattern for Hundredths

Fraction Name	Read the Number	Decimal Name
$\frac{1}{100}$	1 hundredth	0.01
$\frac{5}{100}$	5 hundredths	0.05
$\frac{13}{100}$	13 hundredths	0.13
$\frac{20}{100}$	20 hundredths	0.20

Decimals that have **1** digit after the decimal point are "**tenths.**"

Decimals that have **2** digits after the decimal point are "**hundredths.**"

The pattern continues for thousandths. The fraction $\frac{1}{1,000}$ is written as the decimal 0.001. The fraction $\frac{114}{1,000}$ is written as the decimal 0.114. The fraction name and the decimal name are both read as "114 thousandths." A decimal name that has **3** digits after the decimal is read as **"thousandths."**

EXAMPLE How much of the square is shaded? Give the fraction and decimal names.

The square is divided into 100 equal parts. Each part is $\frac{1}{100}$ of the square. The decimal name for $\frac{1}{100}$ is 0.01 (1 hundredth). 42 squares are shaded.

So $\frac{42}{100}$ of the square is shaded. The decimal name for $\frac{42}{100}$ is 0.42 (42 hundredths).

CHECK YOUR UNDERSTANDING

How much of each square is shaded?
Give the fraction and decimal names.

1.

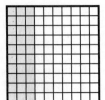

2.

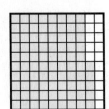

Check your answers on page 293.

Place Value for Decimals

When we write a money amount like $7.29, the number is a decimal. The place that each digit has in the number is very important.

dollars		dimes	pennies
7	•	2	9

The decimal point separates dollars from cents.

The 7 is worth 7 dollars.

The 2 is worth 20 cents, or 2 dimes, or $\frac{2}{10}$ of a dollar.

The 9 is worth 9 cents, or 9 pennies, or $\frac{9}{100}$ of a dollar.

We can use a **place-value chart** to show how much each digit in a decimal is worth. The **place** for a digit is its position in the number. The **value** of a digit is how much it is worth.

EXAMPLE The number 2.345 is shown in a place-value chart below.

1s ones place		0.1s tenths place	0.01s hundredths place	0.001s thousandths place
2	•	3	4	5

The 2 in the ones place is worth 2.

The 3 in the tenths place is worth 0.3 (3 tenths).

The 4 in the hundredths place is worth 0.04 (4 hundredths).

The 5 in the thousandths place is worth 0.005 (5 thousandths).

2.345 is read "2 and 345 thousandths."

The decimal point is read as "and."

Comparing Decimals

A place-value chart can help us to compare two decimal numbers.

EXAMPLE Compare the numbers 5.247 and 5.274.

1s ones place		0.1s tenths place	0.01s hundredths place	0.001s thousandths place
5	•	2	4	7
5	•	2	7	4

Start on the left side.

The ones digits *are* the same. They are both worth 5.

The tenths digits *are* the same. They are worth $\frac{2}{10}$, or 0.2.

The hundredths digits are *not* the same. The 4 is worth $\frac{4}{100}$, or 0.04, and the 7 is worth $\frac{7}{100}$, or 0.07.

So 5.274 is larger than 5.247. $\qquad$ $5.274 > 5.247$

EXAMPLE Which number is larger, 2.4 or 2.40?

The ones digits are the same. The tenths digits are the same.

The hundredths place in the number 2.40 has a 0. It is worth $\frac{0}{100}$, which is 0. So the hundredths place in 2.40 has no value.

2.4 and 2.40 are equal. $2.4 = 2.40$

CHECK YOUR UNDERSTANDING

Which number is larger?

1. 2.37 or 2.7 $\qquad$ **2.** 0.5 or 0.469

3. 0.84 or 0.8 $\qquad$ **4.** 1.7 or 1.09

Check your answers on page 293.

Factors of a Number and Prime Numbers

When two numbers are multiplied, the number answer is called the **product.** The two numbers that are multiplied are called **factors** of the product.

EXAMPLE $3 \times 5 = 15$. 15 is the product of 3 and 5. 3 is a factor of 15. 5 is another factor of 15.

EXAMPLE Find all the factors of 24.

Ways to Write 24	Factors of 24
$1 \times 24 = 24$	1 and 24
$2 \times 12 = 24$	2 and 12
$3 \times 8 = 24$	3 and 8
$4 \times 6 = 24$	4 and 6

The numbers 1, 2, 3, 4, 6, 8, 12, and 24 are all factors of 24.

EXAMPLE Find all the factors of 13. There is only one way to multiply two numbers and get 13. $1 \times 13 = 13$. So 1 and 13 are both factors of 13. And they are the only factors of 13.

A counting number that has exactly two factors is called a **prime number.**
A counting number that has 3 or more factors is called a **composite number.**

thirty-seven SRB **37**

Even and Odd Numbers

- A counting number is an **even number** if 2 is one of its factors.
- A counting number is an **odd number** if it is not an even number.

Facts about the Numbers 1 to 20

Number	Factors	Prime or Composite?	Even or Odd?
1	1	neither	odd
2	1 and 2	prime	even
3	1 and 3	prime	odd
4	1, 2, and 4	composite	even
5	1 and 5	prime	odd
6	1, 2, 3, and 6	composite	even
7	1 and 7	prime	odd
8	1, 2, 4, and 8	composite	even
9	1, 3, and 9	composite	odd
10	1, 2, 5, and 10	composite	even
11	1 and 11	prime	odd
12	1, 2, 3, 4, 6, and 12	composite	even
13	1 and 13	prime	odd
14	1, 2, 7, and 14	composite	even
15	1, 3, 5, and 15	composite	odd
16	1, 2, 4, 8, and 16	composite	even
17	1 and 17	prime	odd
18	1, 2, 3, 6, 9, and 18	composite	even
19	1 and 19	prime	odd
20	1, 2, 4, 5, 10, and 20	composite	even

Negative Numbers

Positive numbers are numbers that are greater than 0. **Negative numbers** are numbers that are less than 0.

The numbers -1, -2, -3, $-\frac{1}{2}$, and -31.6 are all negative numbers. The number -2 is read "negative 2."

The scale on a thermometer often shows both positive and negative numbers. A temperature of $-10°C$ is read "10 degrees below zero."

Many number lines include negative numbers.

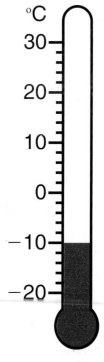

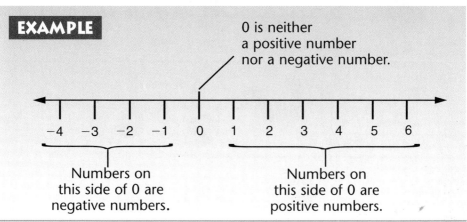

EXAMPLE

0 is neither a positive number nor a negative number.

-4 -3 -2 -1 0 1 2 3 4 5 6

Numbers on this side of 0 are negative numbers.

Numbers on this side of 0 are positive numbers.

A number grid is often shown starting at the number 0. Think of counting backward by 1s on a number grid. Do not stop at 0. The number grid will now include negative numbers.

−19	−18	−17	−16	−15	−14	−13	−12	−11	−10
−9	−8	−7	−6	−5	−4	−3	−2	−1	0
1	2	3	4	5	6	7	8	9	10

EXAMPLE Jack, Paul, and Kevin played marbles. Jack won 7 marbles. Paul lost 2 marbles. Kevin lost 5 marbles.

We can use a number line to show both the gains and the losses. The number line must include both positive and negative numbers.

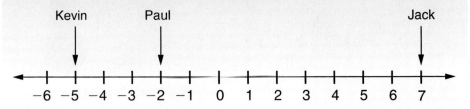

Very Large and Very Small Numbers

Earth weighs about
1,175,800,000,000,000,000,000,000 pounds,
give or take a few billion.
Here is how you say it:
one *septillion,* one hundred
seventy-five *sextillion,*
eight hundred *quintillion*
pounds. A *septillion*
is written with a 1
followed by twenty-four 0s.

There are names for even
larger numbers:

novemdecillion: a 1 followed by sixty 0s
googol: a 1 followed by one hundred 0s

How about this for a tongue twister:
A quintoquadagintillion has one hundred
thirty-eight 0s!

Large numbers of things don't always take up a lot
of space. The blood of a human being contains tiny
cells called *red corpuscles.* There are about 5 million
of these corpuscles in 1 cubic millimeter. This red
square ▪ measures 1 millimeter on each side.

Each side of a cubic millimeter is 1 millimeter long.
The cube takes up very little space.

Try to imagine 5 million tiny cells in a 1-millimeter cube. 1,000 cubic millimeters fit into 1 cubic centimeter, so there are about 5 billion red corpuscles in 1 cubic centimeter. That's a 5 followed by nine 0s, or 5,000,000,000.

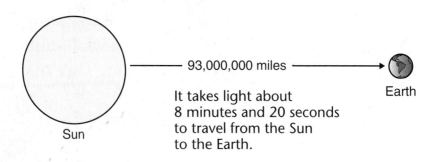

1-centimeter cube

There are almost 1,000 cubic centimeters in 1 quart. The body of a healthy adult contains about 5 quarts of blood. So an adult has about 25 trillion red corpuscles. That's a 25 followed by twelve 0s, or 25,000,000,000,000.

Do you see why we need to have names for very large numbers?

Very small numbers may be even harder to imagine than very large numbers. A beam of light would cover the distance from one side of the classroom to the other in about 0.000000020, or 20 billionths, of a second. Another name for one billionth of a second is a *nanosecond*. Think of it. Light travels about 13 million times as fast as a car.

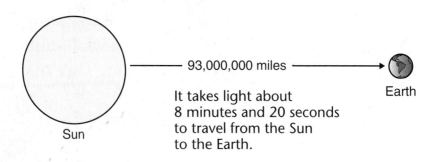

93,000,000 miles

Sun

It takes light about 8 minutes and 20 seconds to travel from the Sun to the Earth.

Earth

Operations & Computation

Basic Facts for Addition and Subtraction

Reading is easier when you know the words by sight. In mathematics, solving problems is easier when you know the basic number facts. Here are some examples of basic addition and subtraction facts:

Basic addition facts:
$6 + 4 = 10$, $0 + 7 = 7$, $3 + 5 = 8$, $9 + 9 = 18$

Basic subtraction facts:
$10 - 6 = 4$, $7 - 7 = 0$, $8 - 5 = 3$, $18 - 9 = 9$

The **facts table** shown below is a chart with rows and columns. It can be used to show *all* of the basic addition and subtraction facts.

Addition/Subtraction Facts Table

+,−	0	1	2	3	4	5	6	7	8	9
0	0	1	2	3	4	5	6	7	8	9
1	1	2	3	4	5	6	7	8	9	10
2	2	3	4	5	6	7	8	9	10	11
3	3	4	5	6	7	8	9	10	11	12
4	4	5	6	7	8	9	10	11	12	13
5	5	6	7	8	9	10	11	12	13	14
6	6	7	8	9	10	11	12	13	14	15
7	7	8	9	10	11	12	13	14	15	16
8	8	9	10	11	12	13	14	15	16	17
9	9	10	11	12	13	14	15	16	17	18

The facts table can be used to find *all* of the basic addition and subtraction facts.

EXAMPLE Which addition facts and subtraction facts can you find using the 4-row and the 6-column?

6-column

+,−	0	1	2	3	4	5	6	7	8	9
0	0	1	2	3	4	5	6	7	8	9
1	1	2	3	4	5	6	7	8	9	10
2	2	3	4	5	6	7	8	9	10	11
3	3	4	5	6	7	8	9	10	11	12
4	4	5	6	7	8	9	10	11	12	13
5	5	6	7	8	9	10	11	12	13	14
6	6	7	8	9	10	11	12	13	14	15
7	7	8	9	10	11	12	13	14	15	16
8	8	9	10	11	12	13	14	15	16	17
9	9	10	11	12	13	14	15	16	17	18

4-row →

Go across the 4-row while you go down the 6-column. This row and column meet at a square that shows the number 10.

The numbers 4, 6, and 10 can be used to write two addition facts and two subtraction facts:

$$4 + 6 = 10$$

$$6 + 4 = 10$$

$$10 - 4 = 6$$

$$10 - 6 = 4$$

Basic Facts for Multiplication and Division

Solving problems is easier when you know the basic number facts. Here are some examples of basic multiplication and division facts:

Basic multiplication facts:

$6 \times 4 = 24$, $10 \times 7 = 70$, $1 \times 8 = 8$, $3 \times 9 = 27$

Basic division facts:

$24 \div 6 = 4$, $70 \div 10 = 7$, $8 \div 1 = 8$, $27 \div 3 = 9$

The **facts table** shown below is a chart with rows and columns. It can be used to find *all* of the basic multiplication and division facts.

Multiplication/Division Facts Table

×,÷	1	2	3	4	5	6	7	8	9	10
1	1	2	3	4	5	6	7	8	9	10
2	2	4	6	8	10	12	14	16	18	20
3	3	6	9	12	15	18	21	24	27	30
4	4	8	12	16	20	24	28	32	36	40
5	5	10	15	20	25	30	35	40	45	50
6	6	12	18	24	30	36	42	48	54	60
7	7	14	21	28	35	42	49	56	63	70
8	8	16	24	32	40	48	56	64	72	80
9	9	18	27	36	45	54	63	72	81	90
10	10	20	30	40	50	60	70	80	90	100

The facts table can be used to find *all* of the basic multiplication and division facts.

EXAMPLE Which multiplication facts and division facts can you write using the 4-row and the 6-column?

6-column

×,÷	1	2	3	4	5	6	7	8	9	10
1	1	2	3	4	5	6	7	8	9	10
2	2	4	6	8	10	12	14	16	18	20
3	3	6	9	12	15	18	21	24	27	30
4	4	8	12	16	20	24	28	32	36	40
5	5	10	15	20	25	30	35	40	45	50
6	6	12	18	24	30	36	42	48	54	60
7	7	14	21	28	35	42	49	56	63	70
8	8	16	24	32	40	48	56	64	72	80
9	9	18	27	36	45	54	63	72	81	90
10	10	20	30	40	50	60	70	80	90	100

4-row →

Go across the 4-row to the 6-column. This row and column meet at a square that shows the number 24.

The numbers 4, 6, and 24 can be used to write two multiplication facts and two division facts:

$$4 \times 6 = 24$$

$$6 \times 4 = 24$$

$$24 \div 4 = 6$$

$$24 \div 6 = 4$$

Fact Triangles and Fact Families

Fact Triangles are tools that can help you memorize the basic facts. One set of Fact Triangles is used to practice addition and subtraction facts. A second set of Fact Triangles is used to practice multiplication and division facts.

Here is a Fact Triangle card. The "+,−" printed on the card means that it is used to practice addition and subtraction facts. The number in the • corner is the sum of the other two numbers.

Fact family for this Fact Triangle

$$8 + 9 = 17 \qquad 9 + 8 = 17$$
$$17 - 8 = 9 \qquad 17 - 9 = 8$$

A Fact Triangle shows basic facts for the numbers. These facts are called a **fact family.**

Work with a partner when you use Fact Triangles to practice facts. One partner covers one of the three corners with a finger. The other partner gives an addition or subtraction fact.

EXAMPLE Here are the ways to use the fact triangle shown above.

Bob covers 17. Alice says "8 + 9 equals 17" or "9 + 8 equals 17."
Bob covers 9. Alice says "17 − 8 equals 9."
Bob covers 8. Alice says "17 − 9 equals 8."

Here is a Fact Triangle card. The "×,÷" printed on the card means that it is used to practice multiplication and division facts. The number in the • corner is the product of the other two numbers.

Fact family for this Fact Triangle

$$5 \times 8 = 40$$
$$8 \times 5 = 40$$
$$40 \div 5 = 8$$
$$40 \div 8 = 5$$

CHECK YOUR UNDERSTANDING

1. Write the fact family for each of these fact triangles.

a.

b.

2. Draw a fact triangle for each of these fact families. Write in the three numbers for each triangle.

a.
$$7 + 5 = 12$$
$$5 + 7 = 12$$
$$12 - 5 = 7$$
$$12 - 7 = 5$$

b.
$$6 \times 10 = 60$$
$$10 \times 6 = 60$$
$$60 \div 6 = 10$$
$$60 \div 10 = 6$$

Check your answers on page 294.

Shortcuts

Here are some ways to use facts you know to learn new facts. They are called shortcuts.

Plus 0: If 0 is added to a number, the number is not changed.
Examples $6 + 0 = 6$ $0 + 812 = 812$

Minus 0: If 0 is subtracted from a number, the number is not changed.
Examples $6 - 0 = 6$ $1,999 - 0 = 1,999$

Times 0: If a number is multiplied by 0, the answer is 0.
Examples $6 \times 0 = 0$ $0 \times 46 = 0$ $1,999 \times 0 = 0$

Times 1: If a number is multiplied by 1, the number is not changed.
Examples $1 \times 6 = 6$ $46 \times 1 = 46$ $1 \times 812 = 812$

Times 5: To multiply by 5, think "nickels."
Example $7 \times 5 = ?$ 7 nickels is 35¢. So $7 \times 5 = 35$.

Times 10: To multiply by 10, think "dimes."
Example $7 \times 10 = ?$ 7 dimes is 70¢. So $7 \times 10 = 70$.

Turn-around shortcut for addition: Numbers have the same sum when they are turned around and added in reverse order.

Turn-around shortcut for multiplication: Numbers have the same product when they are turned around and multiplied in reverse order.

Partial-Sums Addition Method

There are different methods you can use to add.
One of these is called the **partial-sums method.**
It is described below. You may have a favorite
addition method of your own. Even if you do, make
sure that you can also use the partial-sums method.

Here is the partial-sums method for adding 2-digit
or 3-digit numbers:

1. Add the 100s.

2. Add the 10s.

3. Add the 1s.

4. Add the sums you just found (the partial sums).

EXAMPLE   Add 248 + 187 using the partial-sums
method.

		100s	10s	1s
		2	4	8
		+ 1	8	7
Add the 100s.	200 + 100 =	3	0	0
Add the 10s.	40 + 80 =	1	2	0
Add the 1s.	8 + 7 =		1	5
Add the partial sums.	300 + 120 + 15 =	4	3	5

You can use base-10 blocks to show how the partial-sums addition method works.

> **EXAMPLE**   Use base-10 blocks to add 248 + 187.
>
> Each base-10 cube is worth 1.
>
> Each base-10 long is worth 10.
>
> And each base-10 flat is worth 100.
>
> Add the blocks in each column. Then find the total.

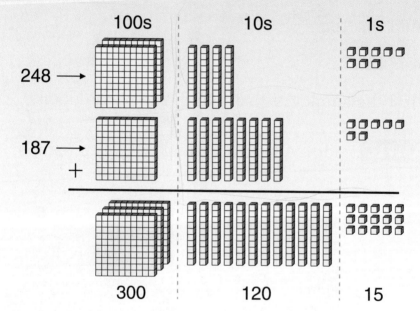

Find the total.   300 + 120 + 15 = 435

Column Addition Method

Many people prefer the **Column Method** for adding.

Here is the Column Method for adding 2-digit or 3-digit numbers:

1. Draw lines to separate the 1s, 10s, and 100s places.

2. Add the numbers in each column. Write each sum in its column.

3. If there are 2 digits in the 1s place, trade 10 ones for 1 ten.

4. If there are 2 digits in the 10s place, trade 10 tens for 1 hundred.

EXAMPLE Add 248 + 187 using the Column Addition Method.

	100s	10s	1s
	2	4	8
	+ 1	8	7
Add each column.	3	12	15

Two digits in the ones place. 15 ones is the same as 1 ten and 5 ones.

	100s	10s	1s
Adjust 1s and 10s.	3	13	5

Two digits in the tens place. 13 tens is the same as 1 hundred and 3 tens.

	100s	10s	1s
Adjust 10s and 100s	4	3	5

248 + 187 = 435

Trade-First Subtraction Method

One method you can use to subtract is called the **trade-first method.** Here is the trade-first method for subtracting 2-digit or 3-digit numbers:

1. Look at the digits in the 10s place. If you cannot subtract these digits without getting a negative number, trade 1 hundred for 10 tens.

2. Look at the digits in the 1s place. If you cannot subtract these digits without getting a negative number, trade 1 ten for 10 ones.

3. Subtract in each column.

EXAMPLE Subtract 164 from 312 using the trade-first method.

100s	10s	1s
3	1	2
− 1	6	4

100s	10s	1s
2	11	
$\cancel{3}$	$\cancel{1}$	2
− 1	6	4

100s	10s	1s
2	10 / $\cancel{1}\!\!\!\!11$	12
$\cancel{3}$	$\cancel{1}$	$\cancel{2}$
− 1	6	4
1	4	8

Look at the 10s place. You cannot remove 6 tens from 1 ten. So trade 1 hundred for 10 tens.

Look at the 1s place. You cannot remove 4 ones from 2 ones. So trade 1 ten for 10 ones.

Now subtract in each column.

EXAMPLE Subtract 324 − 167.

Model the larger number 324.
Think: Can I remove 6 longs from 2 longs? (no)

hundreds	tens	ones
□ □ □	‖	▫▫▫▫
1	6	7

```
  3 2 4
− 1 6 7
```

Trade 1 flat for 10 longs.
Think: Can I remove 7 cubes from 4 cubes? (no)

hundreds	tens	ones
□ □ ○→	‖ ⦅‖‖‖ ‖‖‖⦆	▫▫▫▫
1	6	7

Trade 1 long for 10 cubes.

hundreds	tens	ones
□ □	‖ ‖‖‖‖ ‖‖‖→	▫▫▫▫ ▦▦
1	6	7

After all trading, the blocks look like this:

hundreds	tens	ones
□ □	‖ ‖‖‖‖ ‖‖‖	▫▫▫▫ ▦▦
1	6	7

Subtract in each column. The difference is 157.

hundreds	tens	ones
□	‖ ‖‖‖	▫▫▫▫ ▫▫▫

```
  3 2 4
− 1 6 7
─────────
  1 5 7
```

Left-to-Right Subtraction Method

You can subtract two numbers by subtracting one column at a time. Start with the left column and end with the right column. That is why the method is called **Left-to-Right Method.**

Here is the Left-to-Right Method for subtracting 2-digit or 3-digit numbers:

1. Subtract the 100s.

2. Next subtract the 10s.

3. Then subtract the 1s.

EXAMPLES Use the Left-to-Right Method to solve these problems.

$$
\begin{array}{r} 60 \\ -\ 27 \\ \hline \end{array}
\qquad
\begin{array}{r} 932 \\ -\ 356 \\ \hline \end{array}
$$

There are no hundreds. So subtract the 10s first.

	10s	1s
	6	0
Subtract the 10s. −	2	0
	4	0
Subtract the 1s. −		7
	3	3

	100s	10s	1s
	9	3	2
Subtract the 100s. −	3	0	0
	6	3	2
Subtract the 10s. −		5	0
	5	8	2
Subtract the 1s. −			6
	5	7	6

Counting-Up Subtraction Method

You can subtract two numbers by counting up from the smaller to the larger number. The first step is to count up to the nearest multiple of 10. Then count by 10s and 100s.

Subtracting this way is called the **Counting-Up Method.**

EXAMPLE Subtract 38 from 325 by counting up. First, write the smaller number, 38. Next, count from 38 up to 325. Circle each number that you count up.

```
        3 8
   +      (2)      Count to the nearest 10.
        4 0
   +    (6 0)      Count to 100.
      1 0 0
   + (2 0 0)       Count to the largest
      3 0 0        possible hundred.
   +    (2 5)      Count to the larger
      3 2 5        number.
```

Then, add the numbers you circled.

```
     2
    60
   200
 +  25
   287   You counted up by 287.
```

So 325 − 38 = 287.

Partial-Products Multiplication Method

One way to multiply numbers is called the **partial-products method.** Write 1s, 10s, and 100s above the columns, as shown below.

EXAMPLE Multiply 5 × 26.

Think of 26 as 2 tens and 6 ones.
Then multiply each part of 26 by 5.

	100s	10s	1s
		2	**6**
×			**5**
5 ones × 2 tens: 5 × 20 =	1	0	0
5 ones × 6 ones: 5 × 6 = +		3	0
Add these two parts: 100 + 30 =	**1**	**3**	**0**

EXAMPLE Use an array diagram to show 5 × 26.
There are 5 rows. Each row has 26 dots. Each row
has been divided to show 2 tens and 6 ones.

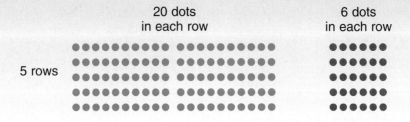

20 dots
in each row

6 dots
in each row

5 rows

Multiply each part: 5 × 20 = 100   5 × 6 = 30
Add these two parts: 5 × 26 = 100 + 30, which is 130.

EXAMPLE Multiply 34 × 26.

Think of 26 as 2 tens and 6 ones.
Think of 34 as 3 tens and 4 ones.
Then multiply each part of 26 by each part of 34, as shown below.

		100s	10s	1s
			2	6
	×		3	4
3 tens × 2 tens:	30 × 20 =	6	0	0
3 tens × 6 ones:	30 × 6 =	1	8	0
4 ones × 2 tens:	4 × 20 =		8	0
4 ones × 6 ones:	4 × 6 = +		2	4
Add these four parts: 600 + 180 + 80 + 24 =		8	8	4

The problem 34 × 26 has been split up into four
easy problems. The answer to each easy problem is
called a **partial product.** Adding these partial
products gives the answer to 34 × 26.

CHECK YOUR UNDERSTANDING

Multiply.

1. 7 × 46

2. 69
× 8

3. 1,795
× 7

4. 78
× 43

Check your answers on page 294.

Lattice Multiplication Method

The **lattice method** for multiplying numbers has been used for hundreds of years. It is very easy to use if you know the basic multiplication facts. Study the examples below.

EXAMPLE Use the lattice method to multiply 3 × 45.

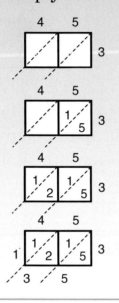

The box with squares and diagonals is called a **lattice**. Write 45 above the lattice. Write 3 on the right side of the lattice.

Multiply 3 × 5.
Write the answer as shown.

Multiply 3 × 4.
Write the answer as shown.

Add the numbers along each diagonal.

3 × 45 = 135

EXAMPLE Use the lattice method. Multiply 6 × 815.

6 × 815 = 4,890

The numbers along a diagonal may add up to a 2-digit number. When this happens ...

- Write the 1s digit.
- Add the 10s digit to the sum in the diagonal above.

EXAMPLE Use the lattice method. Multiply 7 × 89.

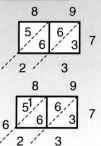

The sum of the numbers in the middle diagonal is 12. Write the 1s digit.

Add 1 to the diagonal above. This sum is 6.

$$7 \times 89 = 623$$

EXAMPLE Use the lattice method. Multiply 34 × 26.

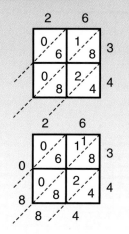

Write 26 above the lattice.
Write 34 on the right side of the lattice.
Multiply 3 × 6. Then multiply 3 × 2.
Multiply 4 × 6. Then multiply 4 × 2.
Write the answers as shown in the lattice.

Add the numbers along each diagonal starting at the right. For the sum 18, add 1 to the diagonal above.

$$34 \times 26 = 884$$

The search for ways to record computation started in India, perhaps about the eleventh century. The lattice method of multiplication was probably passed on from the Hindus to the Arabians, who in turn passed it on to the Europeans. Fifteenth-century writers in western Europe included it in their printed books.

The first printed arithmetic book appeared in Treviso, Italy, in 1478. Luca Pacioli of Italy listed eight different ways to do multiplication in his book called the *Suma*. He called this way "lattice multiplication." The name suggests the gratings placed in Venetian windows to keep people from looking through them.

CHECK YOUR UNDERSTANDING

Copy each lattice. Multiply.

1.

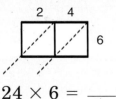

$24 \times 6 =$ ___

2.

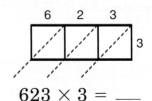

$623 \times 3 =$ ___

3.

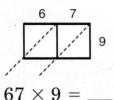

$67 \times 9 =$ ___

4.

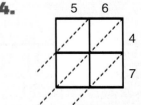

$56 \times 47 =$ ___

Check your answers on page 294.

Arrays

An **array** is a group of objects arranged in **rows** and **columns.**

- The rows and columns are shaped like a rectangle.

- Each row has the same number of objects.

- Each column has the same number of objects.

EXAMPLE The push buttons on a telephone are an array.

The array is shaped like a rectangle.
There are 3 buttons in each row.
There are 4 buttons in each column.

This array is called a 4-by-3 array.

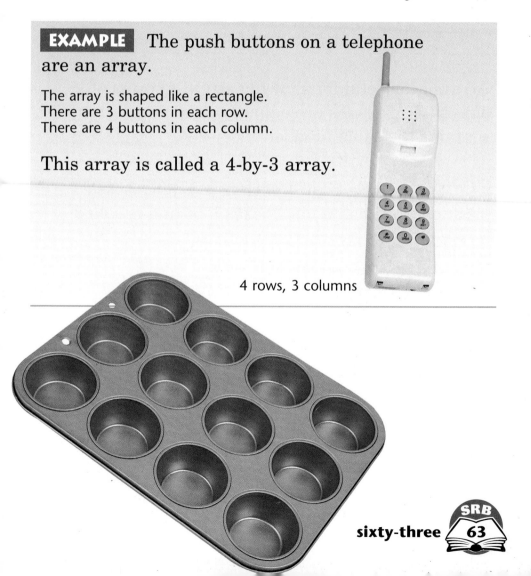

4 rows, 3 columns

EXAMPLE There are 4 different ways to make an array that has 10 objects.

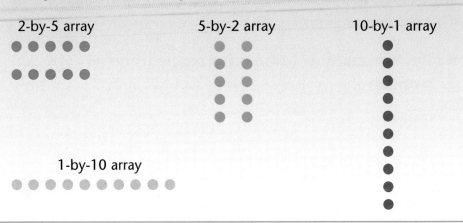

2-by-5 array   5-by-2 array   10-by-1 array

1-by-10 array

Arrays are useful for showing **equal groups** of objects. The groups are equal groups if each group contains the same number of objects.

EXAMPLE Luis buys 4 packages of juice boxes. Each package has 6 juice boxes in it and is called a "six-pack." Show this as an array.

There are 4 groups (4 packages of juice boxes). Each group has the same number of boxes (6) in it.

Draw a 4-by-6 array to show the 4 groups.

Each row stands for 1 package (or six-pack).

Multiplication and Equal Groups

Many number stories are about equal groups.
Equal groups contain the same number of things.

Multiplication is a way to find the total number of
things when you put together equal groups. Multiply
(number of groups) by (number in each group) to
find the total number of things in all the groups.

EXAMPLE Find the total number of dots shown.

One way to find the total number of dots is to count them.
There are 12 dots.

Another way to find the total number of dots is to think of equal
groups of dots. There are 3 groups and 4 dots in each group.

You can write the multiplication sentence $3 \times 4 = 12$ to show that
3 groups of 4 is the same as 12.

There are 12 dots in all.

We say that $3 \times 4 = 12$ is a number model for the
problem. The $\times$ is a **multiplication sign.** Read
3×4 as "3 **times** 4" or as "3 **multiplied by** 4."

Arrays are very useful for showing equal groups of objects. Drawing arrays can help you solve problems involving equal groups.

EXAMPLE   There are 6 cartons with 4 bottles per carton. How many bottles are there in all?

The word **per** means "in each." So, there are 4 bottles in each carton.

The 6 cartons are the 6 groups. Each carton has the same number of bottles (4). So this is an equal-groups problem.

You can draw an array to show the 6 equal groups. Each row stands for 1 carton with 4 bottles in it.

Multiply (number of rows) by (number of columns) to find the total number of objects in the array.

We write 6×4 to show 6 groups of 4.
There are 24 bottles in all.
A number model for the problem is
$6 \times 4 = 24$.

Division and Equal Sharing

An **equal-sharing story** involves dividing a group of things into parts, called *shares*. Equal-sharing stories are also called **division stories.**

Sometimes it is not possible to divide groups into equal shares. The number left over is called the **remainder.**

The **division sign** (÷) is used to show division. It is used in writing number models for equal-sharing stories.

EXAMPLE   Four boys share 24 marbles equally. What is each boy's share?

You can divide the 24 marbles into 4 equal shares.

Each share has 6 marbles. The remainder is 0 because no marbles are left over.

A number model for the problem is 24 ÷ 4 = 6. Read this as "24 divided by 4 equals 6."

EXAMPLE   Four boys share 26 marbles equally. Each share has 6 marbles. The remainder is 2 since 2 marbles are left over. A number model for the problem is 26 ÷ 4 = 6 (remainder 2).

Division and Equal Grouping

Some division stories involve making equal groups of things. The number of things in any one group is known. The problem is to find the number of groups that can be made from the things you have.

> **EXAMPLE** 23 children want to play ball. How many teams can you make with 5 children per team?
>
> The word **per** means "for each."   ⵂⵂⵂ
> So there are 5 children for each team.   ⵂⵂⵂ
> Each team of 5 children is one group.   ⵂⵂⵂ
>
> You can use counters or tallies to find   ⵂⵂⵂ
> how many groups of 5 can be made with   ///
> 23 children.
>
> The tallies above show that 23 children can be divided into 4 groups (teams), with 3 children left over. The remainder is 3.
>
> A number model for this number story is
> $23 \div 5 = 4$ (remainder 3).

Summary for division and equal sharing:
Divide (total) by (number of shares) to find the number in any 1 share.

Summary for division and equal grouping:
Divide (total) by (number in 1 group) to find the number of groups that can be made from the total.

Data & Chance

Tally Charts

There are different ways you can collect information about something.

- Count
- Measure
- Ask questions

- Look at something, and describe what you see

The information you collect is called **data.** You can use a **tally chart** to record and organize data.

EXAMPLE   Mr. Davis asked his students to name their favorite drinks. He recorded their choices in the tally chart below.

Favorite Drinks

Drink	Tallies
Milk	⊬⊬
Chocolate milk	///
Soft drink	⊬⊬ ⊬⊬ /
Apple juice	///
Tomato juice	/
Water	//

Milk (5 votes) is more popular than chocolate milk (3 votes).

Soft drink is the most popular choice (11 votes).

Tomato juice is the least popular choice (1 vote).

CHECK YOUR UNDERSTANDING

1. How many children voted for apple juice?

2. Which drinks are less popular than apple juice?

Check your answers on page 294.

Tally Charts and Line Plots

A **line plot** is another way to organize data and make them easier to understand. The example below shows that line plots are very much like tally charts.

EXAMPLE Mrs. Mack gave her class a 5-word spelling test. Here are the children's scores (the number correct):

Amy 3	Bob 4	Becky 2	Carla 4
Paul 4	Jan 3	Tim 5	Amit 4
Felice 1	Alama 2	Arun 1	Jed 3
Drew 3	Diana 2	Logan 4	Nina 4

The test scores can be organized in a tally chart or in a line plot. Both ways use marks to show how many children got the same number of words correct.

The tally chart uses tally marks.   The line plot uses Xs.

Test Scores

Number Correct	Tallies
0	
1	//
2	///
3	////
4	ＨＨ /
5	/

Test Scores

```
                               X
                               X
                            X  X
Number of         X  X  X
Children    X  X  X  X
            X  X  X  X  X
          +--+--+--+--+--+
          0  1  2  3  4  5
            Number Correct
```

The tally chart and line plot both show that 6 children got 4 words correct.

CHECK YOUR UNDERSTANDING

1. Mr. Davis's class is having a picnic. Class members decided on the day for the picnic by voting.

   The tally chart shows how the class voted.

   ### Votes on Day for a Picnic

Day	Tallies
Mon	~~HHt~~ I
Tue	
Wed	///
Thu	~~HHt~~ //
Fri	~~HHt~~ ////

   a. Which day got the most votes?

   b. Which day got the least votes?

   c. How many children voted for Wednesday?

   d. How many children voted?

2. Mrs. Mack gave some children another 5-word spelling test. Here are the children's scores (the number correct):

   Amy 5   Bob 3   Becky 3   Carla 4   Paul 3

   Tim 5   Amit 5   Felice 1   Alama 4   Arun 5

   Make a line plot to organize the test scores.

Check your answers on page 295.

Describing a Set of Data: The Minimum, Maximum, and Range

If you were asked to describe a certain car, you would probably talk about some of its more important features. You might say, "It is a 2001 midsize car. It is red and has 4 doors. It has 2 front and 2 side air bags. It has been driven about 15,000 miles."

If you were asked to describe a data set, you could mention these features:

- The **minimum** is the smallest number.
- The **maximum** is the largest number.
- The **range** is the difference between the largest and the smallest numbers.

EXAMPLE Devon kept a record of the number of pages he read each day.

Mon	Tue	Wed	Thu	Fri
27	19	12	16	16

maximum (largest) number: 27 pages

minimum (smallest) number: 12 pages

To find the **range**, subtract the smallest number from the largest number. The range is 27 − 12, or 15 pages.

Describing a Set of Data: The Median

The numbers in a set of data are often arranged in order. They can be listed from smallest to largest or from largest to smallest. The **median** is the number in the middle of the list. The median is also known as the **middle number** or the **middle value.**

EXAMPLE What is the median height of these five children?

Amit	Beth	Pauli	Sue	Jan
50 inches	44 inches	47 inches	52 inches	51 inches

List the numbers in order. The middle number is 50.

44	47	**50**	51	52

So the median height is 50 inches.

EXAMPLE What is the median weight of these six children?

List the numbers in order. There are two middle numbers. The median is the number halfway between these middle numbers.

Child	Weight
Nina	42 pounds
Arun	56 pounds
Jack	67 pounds
Avida	54 pounds
May	64 pounds
Bart	58 pounds

42	54	**56**	**58**	64	67

So the median weight is 57 pounds.

Describing a Set of Data: The Mode

When you study a set of data, you may notice that one number or answer occurs most often. The **mode** is the number or answer that occurs most often.

EXAMPLE Devon kept a record of the number of pages he read each day.

Mon	Tue	Wed	Thu	Fri
27	19	12	16	16

The number 16 is listed twice (on Thursday and Friday). The other numbers are listed only one time each.

The mode is 16 pages.

If you make a tally chart or a line plot, the mode is easy to find.

EXAMPLE

Our Class's Favorite Drinks

Drink	Tallies
Milk	ﬀﬀ
Chocolate milk	///
Soft drink	ﬀﬀ ﬀﬀ /
Apple juice	///
Tomato juice	/
Water	//

Scores on a 5-Word Test

```
                            X
                            X
                        X   X
Number of           X   X   X
Children        X   X   X   X
                X   X   X   X   X
              +—+—+—+—+—+—+
              0  1  2  3  4  5
              Number Correct
```

The answer given most often is "soft drink." So the mode is soft drink.

The score most children got is 4. So the mode is 4.

CHECK YOUR UNDERSTANDING

1. Devon kept a record of the number of minutes he did homework each day.

Mon	Tue	Wed	Thu	Fri
40	35	23	41	43

Find the minimum, maximum, and range for this set of data.

2. Here are the points that six basketball players scored:

Player	Points
1	4
2	10
3	5
4	0
5	8
6	5

a. Find the median number of points scored.

b. Find the minimum, maximum, and range for this set of data.

3. Devon kept a record of his math-quiz scores. Here is his list of quiz scores:

6 8 6 9 7 10 8 5 9 9 7 6 8 10 6

What is the mode for these quiz scores?

Check your answers on page 295.

The Mean (Average)

Here are three stacks of pancakes:

| 4 | 6 | 2 |

This is not fair.
One person gets
6 pancakes and
another gets 2.

There are 12 pancakes in all. We can move some pancakes to make the stacks equal. Then each stack will have 4 pancakes.

| 4 | 4 | 4 |

This is fair.
Each person gets
4 pancakes.

We say that 4 is the **mean** number of pancakes in each stack.

Here is how to find the mean:

Step 1: Find the total number of objects in all the groups.

Step 2: Find how many objects would be in each group if the groups were equal.

EXAMPLE John earned $4 and Amy earned $2. What is the mean amount they earned?

John   Amy

Step 1: Find the total: $4 + $2 = $6.

John   Amy

Step 2: Divide the total ($6) by the number of groups (2) to make equal groups:
$6 ÷ 2 = $3.

The mean amount John and Amy earned is $3. If John and Amy share their earnings equally, each will get $3.

EXAMPLE Five children take a hike. Each child carries a backpack. Find the mean weight of their backpacks.

Step 1: Add to find the total weight.
5 + 10 + 10 + 15 + 20 = 60 pounds

Step 2: Divide the total weight (60 pounds) by the number of backpacks (5).
60 pounds ÷ 5 = 12 pounds

The mean (average) weight of the backpacks is 12 pounds. If the children rearrange the items in the backpacks so that all 5 backpacks have the same weight, each backpack will weigh 12 pounds.

CHECK YOUR UNDERSTANDING

1. Alex has 14 model cars. Bob has 18 model cars. David has 16 model cars. What is the mean (average) number of cars that the boys have?

2. Amanda kept a record of her math-quiz scores. What is Amanda's mean score?

Quiz #1	Quiz #2	Quiz #3	Quiz #4
4	10	8	10

Check your answers on page 295.

Bar Graphs

A **bar graph** is a drawing that uses bars to show numbers.

EXAMPLE The bar graph below shows how many children in a Grade 3 class chose certain foods as their favorite foods.

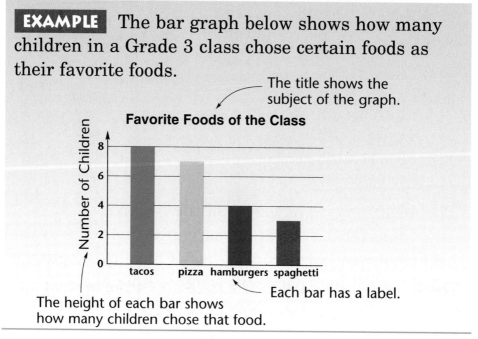

The title shows the subject of the graph.

Each bar has a label.

The height of each bar shows how many children chose that food.

You can answer questions:

How many children chose pizza?

The bar for pizza ends halfway between the line for 6 and the line for 8. So, pizza was the favorite food of 7 children.

You can compare choices:

Eight children chose tacos as their favorite food. Only 3 children chose spaghetti. Tacos are more popular than spaghetti.

When data are collected, sometimes they are put in a tally chart before a bar graph is made.

EXAMPLE The children in a Grade 3 class counted how many pull-ups each of them could do. Their results are shown in the tally chart.

Number of Pull-Ups	Number of Children
0	𝍸 /
1	𝍸
2	////
3	//
4	
5	///
6	/

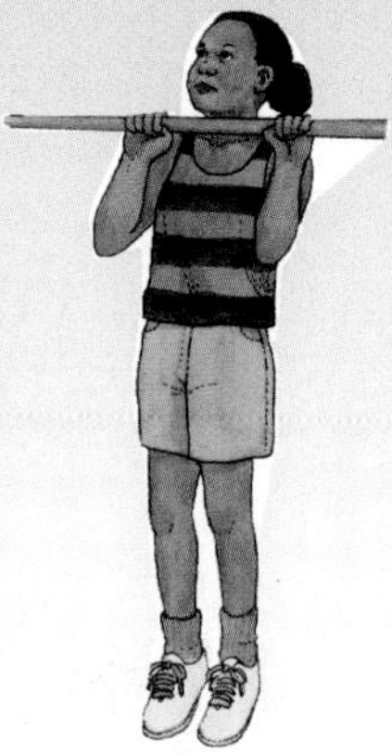

The bar graph below shows the same information as the tally chart, but in a different way.

Pull-Ups by Third Graders

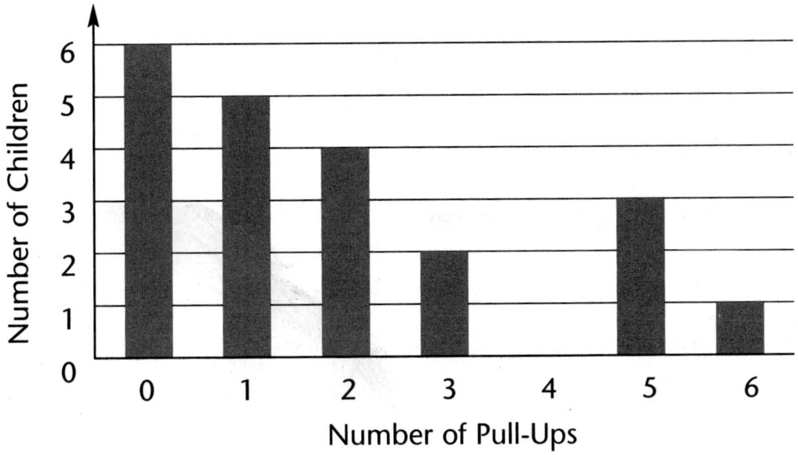

Line Graphs

A line graph is often used to show how something has changed over a period of time.

EXAMPLE At 2:00 P.M. each day for a week, Connie checked her outdoor thermometer and read the temperature. She recorded her information on a line graph.

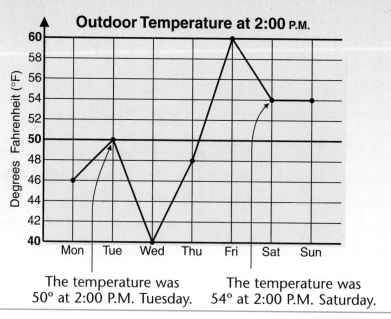

The temperature was 50° at 2:00 P.M. Tuesday.   The temperature was 54° at 2:00 P.M. Saturday.

By carefully reading the graph, you can get much information.

- The graph shows that it was warmer on weekend days (Friday, Saturday, and Sunday) than on other days.

- It was 20 degrees warmer on Friday than it was on Wednesday.

CHECK YOUR UNDERSTANDING

1. Use the line graph on the opposite page to answer the questions.

a. What was the highest temperature?

b. What was the lowest temperature?

c. What days had the same temperature?

d. About what temperature would describe the temperature for the week? Explain your answer.

e. How many days did Connie record the temperature?

2. Nine players played in a baseball game. The table shows how many hits each player made. Make a bar graph to show this information. Copy the following graph on a separate sheet of paper. Then draw the bars.

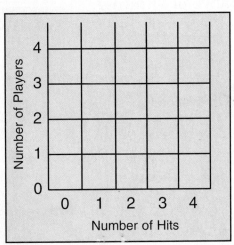

Players	Hits
Carey	4
Jamil	0
Lucy	3
Drew	2
Alica	0
Bev	1
Mel	2
Lee	1
Pete	1

Check your answers on page 295.

Chance and Probability

Things that happen are called **events.** There are many events that you can be sure about.

- You are **certain** that the sun will rise tomorrow.

- It is **impossible** for you to grow to be 12 feet tall.

There are also many events that you *cannot* be sure about.

- You cannot be sure whether it will be sunny or cloudy next Friday.

- You cannot be sure that you will get a letter tomorrow.

You often talk about the **chance** that something will happen. If Bill is a fast runner, you may say, "Bill has a good chance of winning." If Joe is also a fast runner, you may say, "Bill and Joe have the same chance of winning."

Sometimes a number is used to tell the chance of something happening. This number is called a **probability.** It is a number from 0 to 1.

- A probability of 0 means the event is *impossible.* The probability is 0 that you will live to the age of 150.

- A probability of 1 means that the event is *certain* to happen. The probability is 1 that the sun will rise tomorrow.

- A probability of $\frac{1}{2}$ means that an event will happen about half of the time. The probability is $\frac{1}{2}$ that a coin toss will land heads-up. If the coin is tossed many times, it will land heads-up about half the time.

A probability can be written as a fraction, decimal, or percent.

eighty-five

The following examples show some different ways to find probabilities.

EXAMPLE When you toss a tack, it can land with the point up or down.

What is the probability that it will land point up?

One way to find the chance of landing point up is to do an experiment. Toss a large number of tacks and see how many land point up.

Suppose that you toss 100 tacks and 60 land point up. The fraction landing point up is $\frac{60}{100}$. So the probability of landing point up is about $\frac{60}{100}$. $\frac{60}{100}$ can also be written as $\frac{6}{10}$ or 0.6 or 60%.

EXAMPLE A spinner is divided into 3 equal sections. $\frac{1}{3}$ of the spinner is blue. $\frac{1}{3}$ is white. $\frac{1}{3}$ is stripes. What is the probability of landing on blue? On white? On stripes?

The 3 sections have the same size and shape. So we would expect to have the same chance of landing on each section. We say that the chance of landing on any of the 3 sections is **equally likely.**

The blue section is $\frac{1}{3}$ of the spinner. If we spin the spinner many times, we expect to see it land on blue about $\frac{1}{3}$ of the time.

The probability is $\frac{1}{3}$ of landing on blue. There is also a $\frac{1}{3}$ chance of landing on white and a $\frac{1}{3}$ chance of landing on stripes.

Geometry

Points and Line Segments

In mathematics we study numbers. We also study shapes, such as triangles, circles, and pyramids. The study of shapes is called **geometry.**

The simplest shape is a **point.** A point is a location in space. You often make a dot with a pencil to show where a point is. Name the point with a capital letter.

Here is a picture of 3 points. The letter names make it easy to talk about the points. For example, point *A* is closer to point *B* than it is to point *P*. And point *B* is closer to point *A* than it is to point *P*.

A.   .B

•P

A **line segment** is 2 points and the straight path between them. You can use any tool with a straight edge to draw the path between two points.

- The two points are called the **endpoints** of the line segment.

- The line segment is the shortest path between the endpoints.

The symbol for a line segment is a raised bar ——. The bar is written above the letters that name the endpoints of the segment. The following line segment can be written as $\overline{AB}$ or as $\overline{BA}$.

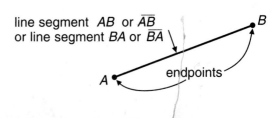

line segment *AB* or $\overline{AB}$
or line segment *BA* or $\overline{BA}$

B

endpoints

A

Rays and Lines

A **ray** is a line segment that goes on forever in *one* direction. You can draw a line segment with 1 arrowhead to stand for a ray.

Point R is the **endpoint** of this ray. The symbol for a ray is a raised bar with one arrowhead $\longrightarrow$. The ray shown here can be written $\overrightarrow{RA}$. The endpoint R is listed first. The second letter names some other point on the ray.

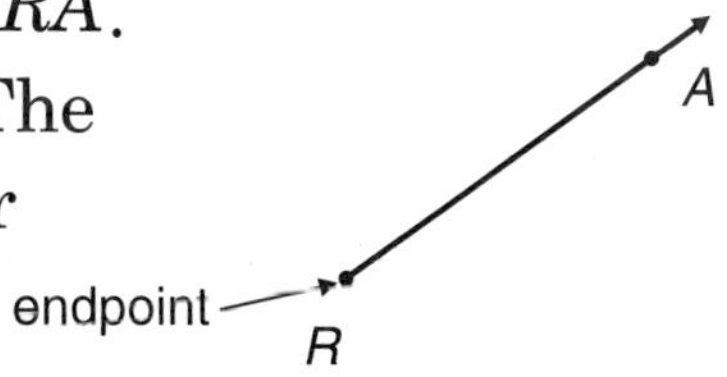

endpoint ⟶

R

A

A **line** is a straight path that goes on forever in *both* directions. You can draw a line segment with 2 arrowheads to stand for a line. The symbol for a line is a raised bar with 2 arrowheads $\longleftrightarrow$.

You can name a line by listing 2 points on the line. Then write the symbol for a line above the letters. The line here is written as $\overleftrightarrow{FE}$ or as $\overleftrightarrow{EF}$.

E

F

EXAMPLE Write all the names for this line.

Points C, A, and T are all on the line. Use any 2 points to write the name of the line.

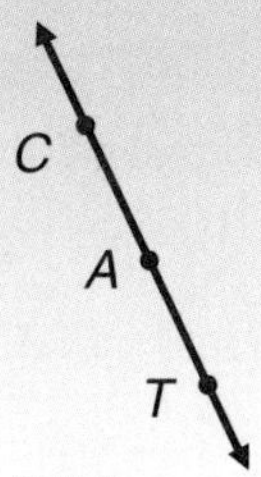

C

A

T

$\overleftrightarrow{CA}$ or $\overleftrightarrow{AC}$ or $\overleftrightarrow{CT}$ or $\overleftrightarrow{TC}$ or $\overleftrightarrow{AT}$ or $\overleftrightarrow{TA}$

Angles

An **angle** is formed by 2 rays or 2 line segments that share the same endpoint.

angle formed by 2 rays   angle formed by 2 segments

The endpoint where the rays or line segments meet is called the **vertex** of the angle. The rays or segments are called the **sides** of the angle.

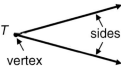

$\angle$ is the symbol for angle. This is angle T, or $\angle T$.

Angles can be measured with an angle measurer (protractor). Angles are measured in degrees. A **right angle** measures 90° (90 degrees). Its sides form a square corner. You often draw a small corner symbol inside the angle to show that it is a right angle.

EXAMPLES The small curved arrow in each picture shows which angle opening should be measured.

 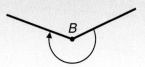 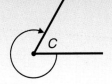

Measure of $\angle A$ is 60°.   Measure of $\angle B$ is 225°.   Measure of $\angle C$ is 300°.

Parallel Lines and Segments

Parallel lines are lines that never meet and are always the same distance apart. Imagine a railroad track that goes on forever. The two rails are parallel. The rails never meet or cross. The rails are always the same distance apart (about 4 ft 8 in.).

Parallel line segments are segments that are always the same distance apart. The top and bottom edges of this page are parallel because they are always the same distance apart (about 9 in.).

The symbol for *parallel* is a pair of vertical lines ||.

If lines or segments cross each other, they **intersect.**

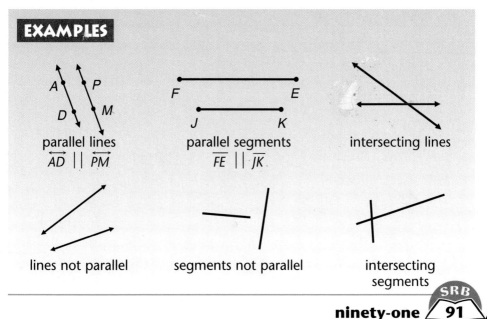

EXAMPLES

parallel lines
$\overleftrightarrow{AD} \parallel \overleftrightarrow{PM}$

parallel segments
$\overline{FE} \parallel \overline{JK}$

intersecting lines

lines not parallel

segments not parallel

intersecting segments

Line Segments, Rays, Lines, and Angles

Figure	Name and Description	Symbol
•A	**point** *A* A location in space.	*A*
F *E* endpoints	**line segment** *EF* or *FE* A straight path between 2 points, called its **endpoints.**	$\overline{EF}$ or $\overline{FE}$
N *M* endpoint	**ray** *MN* A straight path that goes on forever in one direction from an **endpoint.**	$\overrightarrow{MN}$
P *R*	**line** *PR* or line *RP* A straight path that goes on forever in both directions.	$\overleftrightarrow{PR}$ or $\overleftrightarrow{RP}$

Figure	Name and Description	Symbol
vertex *T*	**angle** *T* Two rays or line segments with a common endpoint, called the **vertex**.	$\angle T$
B *A* *S* *R*	**parallel lines** *AB* and *RS* Lines that never meet and that are everywhere the same distance apart. **Parallel line segments** are segments that are the same distance apart.	$\overleftrightarrow{AB} \parallel \overleftrightarrow{RS}$
R *E* *D* *S*	**intersecting lines** *DE* and *RS* Lines that meet. **Intersecting line segments** are segments that meet.	none

Polygons

A **polygon** is a flat 2-dimensional figure made up of 3 or more line segments called **sides.**

- The sides of a polygon are connected end-to-end and make a closed path.

- The sides of a polygon do not cross (intersect).

Each endpoint where two sides meet is called a **vertex.** The plural of *vertex* is *vertices*.

Figures That Are Polygons

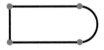

4 sides, 4 vertices

3 sides, 3 vertices

7 sides, 7 vertices

Figures That Are NOT Polygons

All sides of a polygon must be line segments. Curved lines are not line segments.

The sides of a polygon must form a closed path.

A polygon must have at least 3 sides.

The sides of a polygon must not cross.

Polygons are named after the number of sides.
The prefix for a name tells the number of sides.

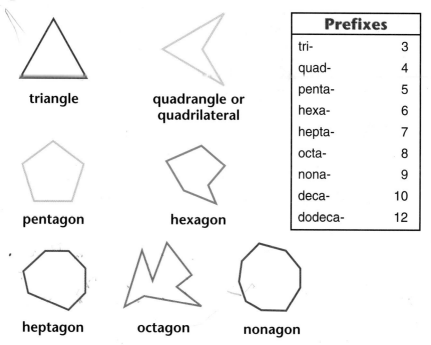

Prefixes	
tri-	3
quad-	4
penta-	5
hexa-	6
hepta-	7
octa-	8
nona-	9
deca-	10
dodeca-	12

triangle

quadrangle or quadrilateral

pentagon

hexagon

heptagon

octagon

nonagon

A **regular polygon** is a polygon whose sides all have the same length and whose angles are all the same size.

The hexagon shown here is a regular hexagon.
All six sides are the same length.
All six angles are the same size.

CHECK YOUR UNDERSTANDING

1. Which of the 7 polygons shown at the top of the page are regular polygons?

2. Name the polygon.

a. 6 sides   b. 4 sides   c. 8 sides   d. 12 sides

Check your answers on page 295.

SRB

Triangles

Triangles are the simplest type of polygon. The prefix "tri" means *three*. All triangles have 3 sides, 3 vertices, and 3 angles.

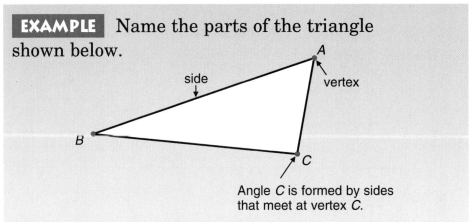

EXAMPLE Name the parts of the triangle shown below.

side

vertex

A

B

C

Angle *C* is formed by sides that meet at vertex *C*.

The sides are $\overline{BC}, \overline{BA},$ and $\overline{CA}$. The sides are the line segments that form the triangle.

The vertices are the points *B*, *C*, and *A*. Each endpoint where two sides meet is called a *vertex*.

The angles are $\angle B$, $\angle C$, and $\angle A$. An angle is formed by the two sides that meet at a vertex. For example, $\angle B$ is formed by $\overline{BC}$ and $\overline{BA}$.

Triangles have 3-letter names. You name a triangle by listing the letters for each vertex in order. The triangle in the example above has 6 possible names:

triangle *BCA, BAC, CAB, CBA, ABC,* or *ACB.*

Triangles have many different sizes and shapes. Two special types of triangles have been given names.

Equilateral Triangles

An **equilateral triangle** is a triangle with all 3 sides the same length. All equilateral triangles have the same shape.

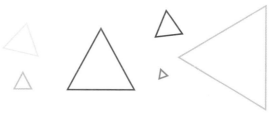

Right Triangles

A **right triangle** is a triangle with one right angle (square corner). Right triangles can have many different shapes.

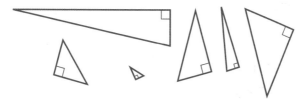

Other triangles are shown below. None of these is an equilateral triangle. None is a right triangle.

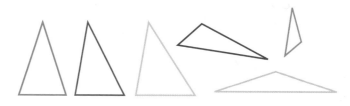

Quadrangles

A **quadrangle** is a polygon that has 4 sides. Another name for *quadrangle* is **quadrilateral.**
The prefix "quad" means *four.* All quadrangles have 4 sides, 4 vertices, and 4 angles.

For the quadrangle shown here:

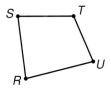

The sides are $\overline{RS}$, $\overline{ST}$, $\overline{TU}$, and $\overline{UR}$.
The vertices are R, S, T, and U.
The angles are $\angle R$, $\angle S$, $\angle T$, and $\angle U$.

Some quadrangles have 2 pairs of parallel sides. These quadrangles are called **parallelograms.**

Reminder: Two sides are parallel if they are everywhere the same distance apart.

Figures That Are Parallelograms

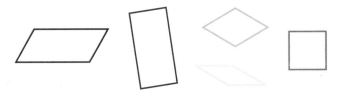

Opposite sides are parallel in each figure.

Figures That Are NOT Parallelograms

No parallel sides.

Only 1 pair of parallel sides.

3 pairs of parallel sides. But a parallelogram must have 4 sides.

Some quadrangles have special names.
Some of them are parallelograms.
Others are not parallelograms.

Quadrangles That Are Parallelograms	
	Rectangles are parallelograms. They have 4 right angles (square corners). The sides of a rectangle do not all have to be the same length.
	Rhombuses are parallelograms. Their 4 sides are all the same length.
	Squares are parallelograms. They have 4 right angles (square corners). Their 4 sides are all the same length. All squares are rectangles. All squares are rhombuses.

Quadrangles That Are NOT Parallelograms	
	Trapezoids have exactly 1 pair of parallel sides. The 4 sides of a trapezoid can all have different lengths.
	A **kite** is a 4-sided polygon with two pairs of equal sides. The equal sides are next to each other. The four sides cannot all have the same length. (So a rhombus is not a kite.)
others	Any closed figure with 4 sides that is not named above.

Circles

A **circle** is a curved line that forms a closed path. All of the points on a circle are the same distance from the **center of the circle.**

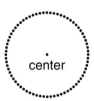

center

Circles are flat 2-dimensional figures. We can draw circles on a sheet of paper.

All circles have the same shape.
But they do not all have the same size.

The size of a circle is the distance across the circle, through its center. This distance is called the **diameter of the circle.**

diameter

EXAMPLE Many pizzas have a circle shape. We often order a size of a pizza by saying the diameter we want.

A "12-inch pizza" means a pizza with a 12-inch diameter.

A "16-inch pizza" means a pizza with a 16-inch diameter.

A 12-inch pizza

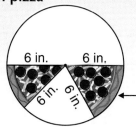

6 in.   6 in.

6 in.   6 in.

The pizza is 12 inches wide.
The diameter is 12 inches.

Each slice is a wedge that has 6-inch long sides.

CHECK YOUR UNDERSTANDING

Use your ruler to measure the diameter of each circle. Measure to the nearest quarter inch.

1.

2.

3.

Check your answers on page 295.

Geometric Solids

Triangles, quadrangles, and circles are flat shapes. They take up a certain amount of area, but they do not take up space. They are flat **2-dimensional** figures. We can draw the figures on a sheet of paper.

Solid objects that take up space are such things as boxes, books, and pails. They are **3-dimensional** objects. Some solids, such as rocks and animals, do not have regular shapes.

Other solids have shapes that are easy to describe using geometric words. We call these solids **geometric solids.**

The **surfaces** on the outside of a geometric solid may be flat or curved, or both. A **flat surface** of a solid is called a **face.**

A cube has 6 faces.

A cylinder has 2 faces and 1 curved surface.

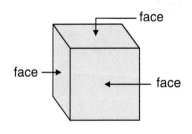

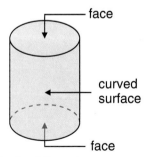

There are 3 other faces that cannot be seen in this picture.

The dashed line shows a hidden edge.

The surfaces of a geometric solid meet one another. They form curves or line segments. These curves or line segments are the **edges** of the solid.

EXAMPLE Identify the edges of a cube and a cylinder.

A cube has 12 edges.   A cylinder has 2 edges.

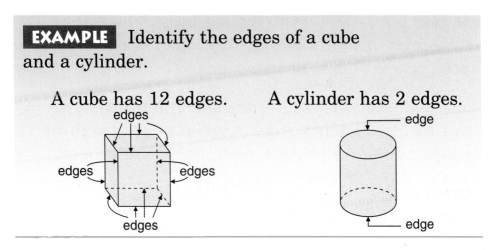

A corner of a geometric solid is called a **vertex.**

EXAMPLE Identify the vertices of a cube, a cylinder, and a cone.

A cube has   A cylinder has ·   A cone has
8 vertices.   0 vertices.   1 vertex.

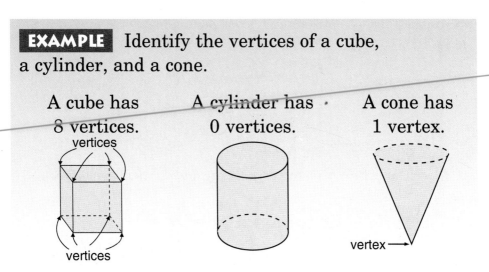

Polyhedrons

A **polyhedron** is a geometric solid whose surfaces are formed by polygons. The faces are all polygons. It does not have any curved surfaces. The faces of a **regular polyhedron** are all copies of one regular polygon that have the same size.

Three important groups of polyhedrons are shown below. These are **pyramids, prisms,** and **regular polyhedrons.** Many polyhedrons do not belong to any of these groups.

Pyramids

triangular pyramids	rectangular pyramids	pentagonal pyramid	hexagonal pyramid

Prisms

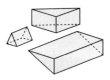 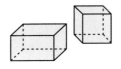

triangular prisms	rectangular prisms	hexagonal prism

Regular Polyhedrons

tetrahedron (pyramid) (4 faces)	cube (prism) (6 faces)	octahedron (8 faces)	dodecahedron (12 faces)	icosahedron (20 faces)

Pyramids

All of the solids below are **pyramids.**

triangular pyramid

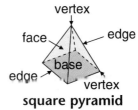

square pyramid

pentagonal pyramid

hexagonal pyramid

Pyramids have flat surfaces called **faces.**

The *shaded* face of each pyramid above is called the **base** of the pyramid. The faces that are not bases all have the shape of a triangle.

The shape of the base is used to name a pyramid. If the base is the shape of a triangle, the pyramid is called a **triangular pyramid.** If the base is a square, the pyramid is called a **square pyramid.**

The pyramids of Egypt have square bases. They are called square pyramids.

Prisms

All of the solids below are **prisms.**

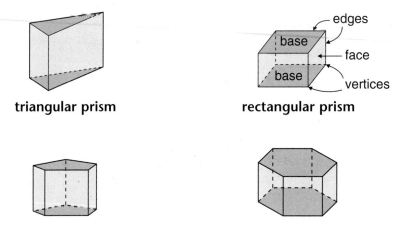

triangular prism

rectangular prism

pentagonal prism

hexagonal prism

Prisms have flat surfaces called **faces.**

The two shaded faces of each prism above are called the **bases** of the prism.

*   Both bases have the same size and shape.

*   Both bases are parallel. This means that the bases are everywhere the same distance apart.

*   The faces that connect the bases are shaped like rectangles or parallelograms.

The shape of the bases is used to name a prism. If the bases are triangles, the prism is called a **triangular prism.** If the bases are rectangles, the prism is called a **rectangular prism.**

Cylinders and Cones

A **cylinder** has two flat surfaces that are connected by a curved surface. Soup cans and paper towel rolls are shaped like cylinders.

The flat surfaces are called **bases.**

- The 2 bases are circles. These circles are the same size.

- The 2 bases are parallel. This means that the bases are everywhere the same distance apart.

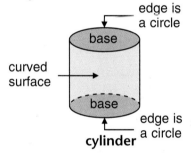

Another solid with a curved surface is a **cone.** Ice cream cones and some paper cups are shaped like cones.

A cone has 1 flat surface with a circle shape. This is the **base** of the cone. The other surface of the cone is a curved surface. The curved surface wraps around the base. It ends at a point called the **apex** of the cone.

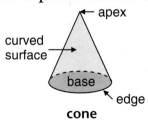

Spheres

A **sphere** is a solid with a curved surface that is shaped like a ball or a globe. All of the points on the sphere's surface are the same distance from the **center of the sphere.**

Spheres are 3-dimensional objects. They take up space. All spheres have the same shape. But not all spheres have the same size.

The size of a sphere is the distance across the sphere and through its center. This distance is called the **diameter of the sphere.**

The segment, $\overline{RS}$, passes through the center of the sphere. The length of this segment is the diameter of the sphere.

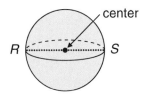

EXAMPLE The Earth is shaped very nearly like a sphere. The diameter of the Earth is about 8,000 miles. The distance from the Earth's surface to the center of the Earth is about 4,000 miles. Every point on the Earth's surface is about 4,000 miles from the center of the Earth.

Layers inside the Earth

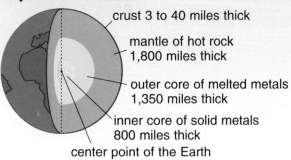

crust 3 to 40 miles thick

mantle of hot rock
1,800 miles thick

outer core of melted metals
1,350 miles thick

inner core of solid metals
800 miles thick

center point of the Earth

Congruent Figures

Sometimes figures have the same shape and same size. We say that these figures are **congruent.** Figures are congruent if they match exactly when one figure is placed on top of the other.

Line segments are congruent if they have the same length.

EXAMPLE Line segments $\overline{AB}$ and $\overline{CD}$ are both 3 cm long.

They have the same shape.
They have the same length.

The line segments are congruent. They match exactly when one segment is placed on top of the other.

Angles are congruent if they have the same degree measure.

EXAMPLE Angle M and angle N are both right angles.

$\angle M$ and $\angle N$ have the same shape.
They each measure 90°.

The angles are congruent. They match exactly when one angle is placed on top of the other.

Circles are congruent if their diameters are the same length.

> **EXAMPLE** The circles here have $\frac{1}{2}$-inch diameters.
>
> They have the same shape.
> They have the same size.
>
>
>
> The circles are congruent. They match exactly when one is placed on top of the other.

If we use a copy machine to copy a figure, the original and the copy are congruent.

> **EXAMPLE** A copy machine was used to copy the pentagon *RSTUV*.
>
> If we cut out the copy, it will match exactly when placed on top of the original.
>
>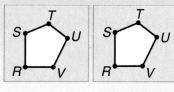
>
> The sides will match exactly.   original   copy
> All the angles will match exactly.

CHECK YOUR UNDERSTANDING

Which one of the following triangles is NOT congruent to the other three?

A   B   C   D

Check your answers on page 296.

Line Symmetry

Look at this cartoon face. A dashed line is drawn through it. The line divides the figure into two parts. Both parts look exactly alike, but are facing in opposite directions.

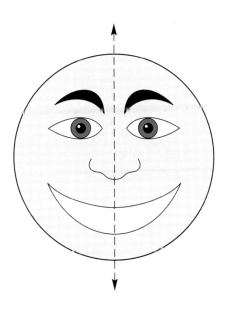

The figure is **symmetric about a line.** The dashed line is called a **line of symmetry** for the figure.

An easy way to find out whether a figure has line symmetry is to fold it in half. If the two halves match exactly, then the figure is symmetric. And the fold line is the line of symmetry.

EXAMPLE The letters T, V, E, and X are symmetric. The lines of symmetry are drawn below for each letter.

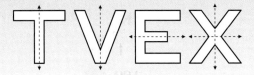

The letter X has two lines of symmetry. You can fold along either line, and the two halves will match exactly.

The figures below are all symmetric. The line of symmetry is drawn for each figure. If there is more than one line of symmetry, they are all drawn.

Figures That Are Symmetric about a Line

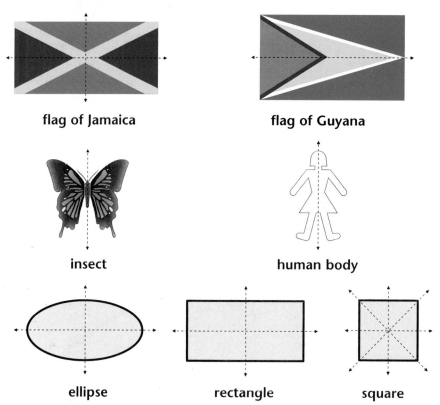

flag of Jamaica

flag of Guyana

insect

human body

ellipse

rectangle

square

CHECK YOUR UNDERSTANDING

1. Trace each pattern-block shape onto a sheet of paper. Draw all lines of symmetry for each shape.

2. How many lines of symmetry does a circle have?

Check your answers on page 296.

Measurement

Measurement Before the Invention of Standard Units

People measured length and weight long before they had rulers and scales. In the past, people used parts of their bodies to measure lengths. Here are some units of length that were based on the human body:

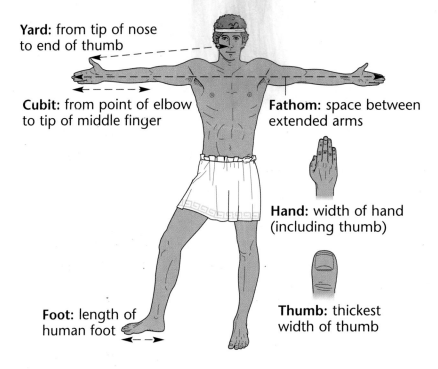

Yard: from tip of nose to end of thumb

Cubit: from point of elbow to tip of middle finger

Fathom: space between extended arms

Hand: width of hand (including thumb)

Foot: length of human foot

Thumb: thickest width of thumb

Look carefully. You will see that a fathom is about the same length as a person's height.

The problem with using body measures is that they are different for different people.

Using **standard units** of length solves this problem. The standard units never change. They are the same for everyone.

If two people measure the same object using standard units, their measurements will be the same or almost the same

The Metric System

About 200 years ago, the **metric system** of measurement was developed. The metric system uses standard units for measuring length, weight, and temperature.

- The standard unit for length is the **meter.** The word *meter* is abbreviated **m.** A meter is about the length of a big step, or the width of a front door.

- The standard unit for weight is the **gram.** The word *gram* is abbreviated **g.** A dime weighs about 2 grams. A paper clip weighs about $\frac{1}{2}$ gram

- The standard unit for temperature is the **Celsius degree** or **°C.** Water freezes at 0°C. Room temperature is usually about 20°C.

The metric system is used all over the world. The United States is the only large country in which the metric system is not used for everyday measurements. We often use the **U.S. customary system** instead. The U.S. customary system uses standard units like the **inch, foot, yard,** and **pound.**

Scientists almost always measure using the metric system. Metric units are often used in sports, such as track and field, ice skating, and swimming. Many food labels include metric measurements.

The metric system is easy to use because it is a decimal system. It is based on the numbers 10, 100, and 1,000.

Let's see what this means by looking at a **meterstick.** A meterstick is a ruler that is 1 meter long. There are probably metersticks in your classroom.

EXAMPLE Part of a meterstick is shown below. It has been divided into smaller units.

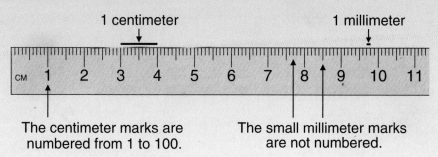

1 centimeter

1 millimeter

The centimeter marks are numbered from 1 to 100.

The small millimeter marks are not numbered.

The meterstick is divided into 100 equal sections. The length of each section is called a **centimeter.** There are 100 centimeters in 1 meter.

Each centimeter is divided into 10 equal sections. The length of each small section is called a **millimeter.** There are 10 millimeters in 1 centimeter. There are 1,000 millimeters in 1 meter.

The U.S. customary system is not based on the numbers 10, 100, and 1,000. This makes it more difficult to use than the metric system. For example, to change inches to yards, you must know that 36 inches equals 1 yard.

CHECK YOUR UNDERSTANDING

1. a. How many centimeters equal 1 meter?

   b. How many millimeters equal 1 centimeter?

   c. How many millimeters equal 1 meter?

2. Which units in the list below are units in the metric system?

foot	millimeter	pound	inch
gram	meter	centimeter	yard

3. a. Draw a line segment that is 4 centimeters long.

   b. Draw another line segment that is 40 millimeters long.

   c. Which line segment is longer?

Check your answers on page 296.

Measuring Length in Centimeters and Millimeters

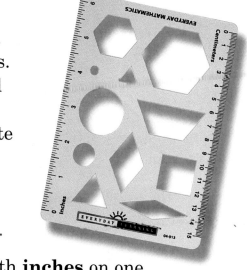

Length is the measure of a distance between two points. Length is usually measured with a ruler. The edges of your Pattern-Block Template are rulers. Tape measures, yardsticks, and metersticks are rulers that are used for measuring longer distances.

Rulers are often marked with **inches** on one side and **centimeters** on the other side. The side showing centimeters is called the **centimeter scale.** The side showing inches is called the **inch scale.**

Each centimeter is divided into 10 equal parts called **millimeters.** A millimeter is $\frac{1}{10}$ or 0.1 of a centimeter. The word *centimeter* is abbreviated **cm.** The word *millimeter* is abbreviated **mm.**

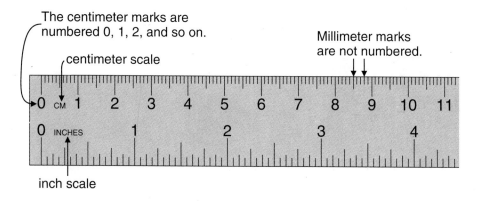

The centimeter marks are numbered 0, 1, 2, and so on.

centimeter scale

Millimeter marks are not numbered.

inch scale

EXAMPLE How long is the rectangle?

Always line up the end of the object with the 0-mark of the ruler.

The end of the rectangle is at the 3-centimeter mark.

The rectangle is 3 centimeters long.
We write this as 3 cm.

If the 0-mark is at the end of a ruler, then the number "0" may not be printed on the ruler. When this happens, line up the end of the object with the end of the ruler.

EXAMPLE How many millimeters long is the arrow?

The 0-mark is at the end of the ruler. Line up the end of the object with the end of the ruler.

There are 40 millimeters from the end of the ruler to the 4 cm mark. The arrow tip is another 5 millimeters past the 4 cm mark.

So the arrow is 45 millimeters long.
We write this as 45 mm.

EXAMPLE Find the length of the needle.

Use centimeters:
The end of the needle is 7 small spaces past the
2 cm mark. Each small space is $\frac{1}{10}$ of a centimeter.

So the needle is $2\frac{7}{10}$ (or 2.7) cm long.

Use millimeters:
There are 20 millimeters from the end of the ruler to the 2 cm mark.
The needle tip is another 7 millimeters past the 2 cm mark.

So the needle is 27 mm long.

EXAMPLE Draw a line segment that is
7.8 centimeters long.

Each centimeter equals 10 millimeters.
So 0.1 cm equals 1 mm, and 0.8 cm = 8 mm.

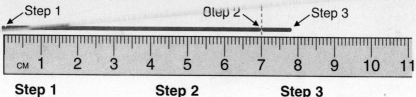

Step 1	**Step 2**	**Step 3**
Make a dot above the end of the ruler.	Draw a line up to the 7 cm mark.	Keep drawing until you have covered 8 more mm spaces.

Changing Units of Length in the Metric System

The basic unit of length in the metric system is the **meter.** We measure smaller lengths using **centimeters** and **millimeters.** We measure longer distances using **kilometers.** The table below shows how these different units of length compare.

Comparing Metric Units of Length		Abbreviations for Units of Length
1 cm = 10 mm	1 mm = $\frac{1}{10}$ cm	mm = millimeter
1 m = 100 cm	1 cm = $\frac{1}{100}$ m	cm = centimeter
1 m = 1,000 mm	1 mm = $\frac{1}{1,000}$ m	m = meter
1 km = 1,000 m	1 m = $\frac{1}{1,000}$ km	km = kilometer

You can use this reference table to change from one metric unit to another. For example, if you know a length in kilometers, you can change it to meters. All changes use the numbers 10, 100, and 1,000.

EXAMPLE Jodi ran a 5-kilometer race. One kilometer equals 1,000 meters. So 5 kilometers is $5 \times 1,000$ or 5,000 meters.

EXAMPLE Mark is 150 cm tall. 100 centimeters is equal to 1 meter. 50 centimeters is $\frac{1}{2}$ meter. So 150 cm = 1 meter + $\frac{1}{2}$ meter, which is 1.5 meters.

Personal References for Metric Units of Length

Sometimes you may not have a ruler or meterstick handy. When this happens, you can estimate lengths by using the lengths of common objects and distances you know. Some examples are given below.

Personal References for Metric Units of Length

About 1 millimeter	About 1 centimeter
Thickness of a dime	Thickness of a crayon
Thickness of a thumbtack point	Width of the head of a thumbtack
Thickness of a paper match (the thin edge)	Thickness of a pattern block

About 1 meter	About 1 kilometer
Width of a door	1,000 big steps (for an adult)
One big step (for an adult)	Length of 10 football fields
Height of a kitchen counter	

The personal references for 1 meter can also be used for 1 yard. One meter is slightly longer than 39 inches. One yard equals 36 inches. So a meter is about 3 inches longer than a yard.

meterstick

yardstick

CHECK YOUR UNDERSTANDING

1. A 10K race is a 10-kilometer race. How many meters are in 10 kilometers?

2. **a.** 3 meters is how many centimeters?

   b. 3.5 meters is how many centimeters?

3. 70 mm is the same length as how many cm?

4. Would you measure the length of your classroom in meters or millimeters?

5. **a.** 2,000 big steps by a man is about how many kilometers?

   b. About how many meters is that?

6. Ann made a stack of dimes using 25 dimes. About how many centimeters high is the stack?

Check your answers on page 296.

Measuring Length in Inches

Length is the measure of a distance between two points. In the U.S. customary system, a standard unit of length is the **inch.** The word *inch* is abbreviated **in.**

On rulers, inches are usually divided into halves, quarters (or fourths), eighths, and sixteenths. The marks to show fractions of an inch are usually different sizes.

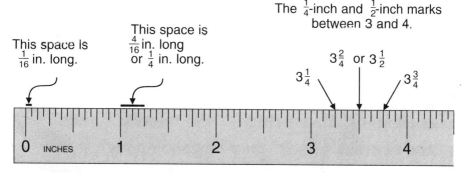

This space is $\frac{1}{16}$ in. long.

This space is $\frac{4}{16}$ in. long or $\frac{1}{4}$ in. long.

The $\frac{1}{4}$-inch and $\frac{1}{2}$-inch marks between 3 and 4.

$3\frac{1}{4}$ $3\frac{2}{4}$ or $3\frac{1}{2}$ $3\frac{3}{4}$

EXAMPLES What is the length of each nail?

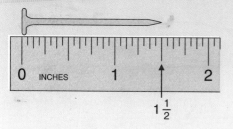

$1\frac{1}{2}$

The end of the nail is at the $1\frac{1}{2}$-inch mark.

The nail is $1\frac{1}{2}$ inches long.

We can write this as $1\frac{1}{2}$ in.

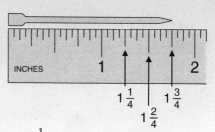

$1\frac{1}{4}$ $1\frac{3}{4}$

$1\frac{2}{4}$

The $\frac{1}{4}$-inch marks between 1 and 2 are shown. The end of the nail is at the $1\frac{3}{4}$-inch mark.

It is $1\frac{3}{4}$ in. long.

EXAMPLE What is the length of the match?

Always line up the end of the object with the 0-mark of the ruler.

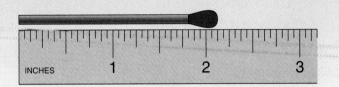

If the 0-mark is at the end of a ruler, the number "0" may not be printed on that ruler.

There are 2 small spaces between the 2-inch mark and the match tip. Each space is $\frac{1}{16}$ inch long.

So the match is $2\frac{2}{16}$ inches long. Because $\frac{2}{16} = \frac{1}{8}$, the length can be written as $2\frac{2}{16}$ inches, or $2\frac{1}{8}$ inches.

There are times when you do not need an exact measurement. Measuring to "the nearest $\frac{1}{2}$ inch" or "the nearest $\frac{1}{4}$ inch" may be good enough.

EXAMPLE Find the length of the pencil to the nearest quarter-inch.

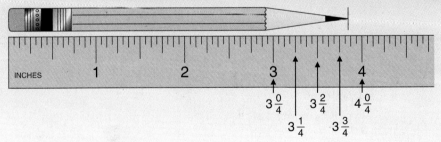

$3\frac{0}{4}$ $3\frac{2}{4}$ $4\frac{0}{4}$

$3\frac{1}{4}$ $3\frac{3}{4}$

The quarter-inches between 3 and 4 are written below the ruler. The tip of the pencil is closest to $3\frac{3}{4}$.

The pencil is $3\frac{3}{4}$ inches long, to the nearest quarter-inch.

CHECK YOUR UNDERSTANDING

1. Draw a line segment that is $2\frac{3}{4}$ inches long.

2. Measure the length of the clothespin to the nearest quarter-inch.

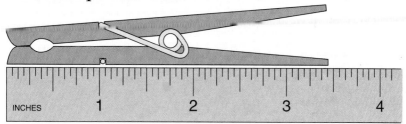

3. Name the measure shown by each letter.

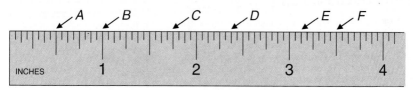

a. A is $\frac{1}{2}$ in. **b.** B is _?_ in. **c.** C is _?_ in.

d. D is _?_ in. **e.** E is _?_ in. **f.** F is _?_ in.

Check your answers on page 296.

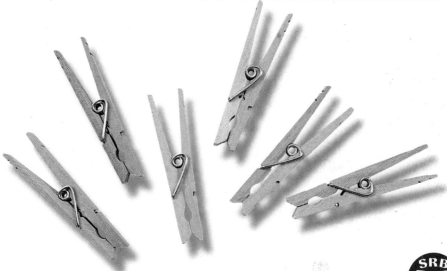

Changing Units of Length in the U.S. Customary System

A basic unit of length in the U.S. customary system is the inch. But we measure length using other units, too. Feet and yards are also used to measure smaller lengths. Miles are used to measure longer distances. The table below shows how different units of length compare.

Comparing U.S. Customary Units of Length		Abbreviations for Units of Length
1 foot = 12 inches	1 inch = $\frac{1}{12}$ foot	in. = inch
1 yard = 3 feet	1 foot = $\frac{1}{3}$ yard	ft = foot
1 yard = 36 inches	1 inch = $\frac{1}{36}$ yard	yd = yard
1 mile = 5,280 feet		mi = mile

You can use this reference table to change from one unit to another. If you know a length in feet, you can change this length to inches. If you know a length in inches, you can change this length to feet. Study the examples on the following page.

EXAMPLE   4 yards is equal to how many feet?

One yard equals 3 feet.

So 4 yards is 4×3, or 12 feet.

EXAMPLE   Lucy is 5 feet 2 inches tall. What is Lucy's height in inches?

One foot is 12 inches.
So 5 feet is 5×12, or 60 inches.

5 feet + 2 inches is the same as
60 inches + 2 inches, which is 62 inches.

Lucy is 62 inches tall.

EXAMPLE   Ari used 24 inches of string to wrap a package. How many feet of string did he use?

One inch is equal to $\frac{1}{12}$ foot. Twenty-four inches will equal $\frac{24}{12}$ feet.
And $\frac{24}{12} = 2$.

So Ari used 2 feet of string.

EXAMPLE   A box is 8 inches long. How many feet long is the box?

One inch is equal to $\frac{1}{12}$ foot. Eight inches is equal to $\frac{8}{12}$ foot. And $\frac{8}{12} = \frac{2}{3}$.

So the box is $\frac{2}{3}$ foot long.

Personal References for U.S. Units of Length

Sometimes you may not have a ruler or yardstick handy. You can estimate lengths by using the lengths of common objects and distances you know. Some examples are given below.

Personal References for U.S. Customary Units of Length

About 1 inch	About 1 foot
Length of a paper clip	Man's shoe length
Width of a quarter	Length of a license plate
Width of a man's thumb	Length of your math journal
About 1 yard	**About 1 mile**
Width of a door	2,000 big steps (for an adult)
One big step (for an adult)	15 football fields (with end zones)
Height of a kitchen counter	

yardstick

1 foot ruler

EXAMPLE Jack's dad measured the length of the basketball court by taking 30 big steps. About how many feet long is the court?

One big step for an adult is about 1 yard. So the basketball court is about 30 yards long. One yard equals 3 feet.

So the court is about 3 × 30, or 90 feet long.

CHECK YOUR UNDERSTANDING

1. a. 7 yards = __?__ feet   **b.** 2 ft = __?__ in.

   c. 6 feet = __?__ yards   **d.** __?__ in. = 2 yd

2. Ari is 4 feet 9 inches tall. What is Ari's height in inches?

3. A man's shoe is about as long as __?__ paper clips.

4. 100 big steps for a man is about __?__ yards.

   About how many feet is that?

5. Jack's uncle walked around the lake. His walk took about 12,000 steps. About how far did he walk?

Check your answers on page 296.

Perimeter

Sometimes we want to know the **distance around** a shape. The distance around is called the **perimeter** of the shape. To measure perimeter, we use units of length like inches or meters or miles.

EXAMPLE Dori rode her bicycle once around the edge of a lake.

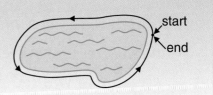

The distance around the lake is 2.3 miles. We say that the perimeter of the lake is 2.3 miles.

To find the perimeter of a polygon, add the lengths of its sides. Always remember to name the unit of length used to measure the shape.

EXAMPLE Jon ran once around the block. How far did he run?

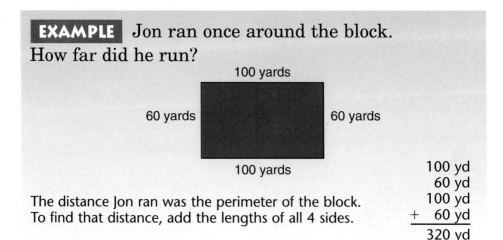

The distance Jon ran was the perimeter of the block. To find that distance, add the lengths of all 4 sides.

```
  100 yd
   60 yd
  100 yd
+  60 yd
  320 yd
```

Jon ran 320 yards.

EXAMPLE Find the perimeter of this square.

All 4 sides have the same length.
The picture shows that a side is
2 centimeters long.

Add the lengths of the sides.
2 cm + 2 cm + 2 cm + 2 cm = 8 cm

The perimeter of the square is 8 cm.

CHECK YOUR UNDERSTANDING

Find the perimeter of the triangle and
the square below.

1.

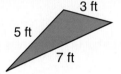

5 ft
3 ft
7 ft

2.

15 mm

3. Measure the sides of your math journal to the
nearest half-inch. What is the math journal's
perimeter?

Check your answers on page 296.

Circumference and Diameter

The perimeter of a circle is the **distance around** the circle.

The perimeter of a circle has a special name. It is called the **circumference** of the circle.

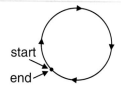

start

end

The top of the soup can shown here is a circle.

The circumference of the circle can be measured with a tape measure.

Wrap the tape measure around the can once. Then read the mark that touches the end of the tape.

The circumference of the can top is how far a can opener turns in opening the can.

The **diameter** of a circle is the distance across the center of a circle.

If you know the diameter, there is a simple rule for estimating the circumference.

Circle Rule: The circumference of a circle is just a little more than 3 times the length of the diameter.

EXAMPLE The diameter of a bicycle wheel is 24 inches. Estimate the circumference of the wheel.

Use the Circle Rule.

24 inches

The circumference is a little more than 3 × 24, or 72 inches.

Suppose the bicycle tire was cut and laid out flat. It would be slightly longer than 72 inches.

CHECK YOUR UNDERSTANDING

1. Measure the diameter of the nickel in millimeters.

2. About how many millimeters is the circumference of the nickel?

3. A 12-inch pizza has a diameter of 12 inches. About how many inches is the distance around the pizza?

Check your answers on page 297.

Area

Sometimes we want to know the amount of **surface inside** a shape. The amount of surface inside a shape is called the **area** of the shape.

One way to find the area of a shape is to count the number of squares of a certain size that cover the inside of the shape.

The rectangle below is covered by squares that are 1 centimeter on each side. Each square is called a **square centimeter.**

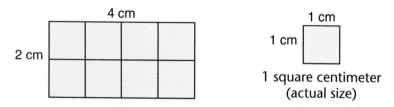

1 square centimeter
(actual size)

Eight of the squares cover the rectangle. The area of the rectangle is 8 square centimeters.

A square with sides 1 inch long is a **square inch.**

A square with 1-foot sides is a **square foot.**

The **square yard** and **square meter** are larger units of area. They are used to measure large areas, such as the area of a floor.

1 square inch
(actual size)

EXAMPLES Count the square units to find the areas of these shapes.

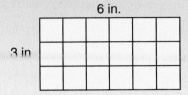

6 in.

3 in

Each square is 1 square inch.
18 squares cover the rectangle.

The area of the rectangle is 18 square inches.

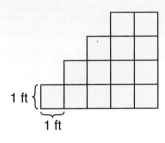

1 ft {

1 ft

Each square is 1 square foot.
14 squares cover the shape.

The area of the shape is 14 square feet.

Remember:

Perimeter is the **distance around** a shape.

Area is the amount of **surface inside** a shape.

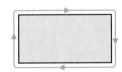

Perimeter is distance around   Area is amount of surface inside

Some surfaces are too large to cover with squares. It would take too long to count a large number of squares.

To find the area of a rectangle, you do not need to count all of the squares that cover it. The example below shows a shortcut for finding the area.

EXAMPLE Find the area of this rectangle.

Each square is 1 square foot.

- There are 4 rows of squares.
- Each row has 10 squares.
- So there are 4 × 10, or 40 squares in all.

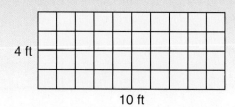

4 ft

10 ft

The area is 40 square feet.

Summary: To find the area of a rectangle:

1. Count the number of rows.

2. Count the number of squares in 1 row.

3. Multiply:

(number of rows) × (number of squares in 1 row)

CHECK YOUR UNDERSTANDING

Find the area of each rectangle.

1. 2 cm

7 cm

2. 3 in.

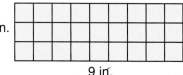

9 in.

3. Which area is larger, 1 square yard or 1 square meter?

Check your answers on page 297.

Volume

Sometimes we want to know the amount of **space inside** a 3-dimensional object. The amount of space inside an object is called the **volume** of the object. Think of volume as the amount of something a box can hold.

We can find the volume of an object by counting the number of cubes of a certain size that would fill the object. To measure the volume of a box, we could fill it with small base-10 cubes.

A base-10 cube has sides that are 1 centimeter long. It is called a **cubic centimeter.** Stack the cubes in the box so that there are no gaps. The volume of the box is the number of cubes needed to fill it.

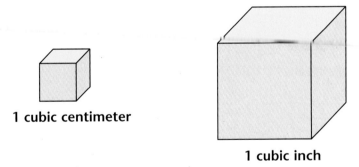

1 cubic centimeter

1 cubic inch

Other cube sizes can be used to measure volume.

A cube with 1-inch sides is called a **cubic inch.**

A cube with 1-foot sides is called a **cubic foot.**

A cube with 1-yard sides is called a **cubic yard.**

A cube with 1-meter sides is called a **cubic meter.**

EXAMPLE Count cubes to find the volumes of these objects.

Each cube is 1 cubic centimeter.
There are 4 cubes.

Object A

The volume is 4 cubic centimeters.

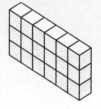

Each cube is 1 cubic centimeter.
There are 4 cubes.

Object B

The volume is 4 cubic centimeters.

Each cube is 1 cubic foot.
There are 18 cubes.

Object C

The volume is 18 cubic feet.

Objects with different shapes can have the same volume. Objects A and B have different shapes, but they have the same volume.

Sometimes objects are too large to fill with cubes. It would take too long to count a large number of cubes.

A **rectangular prism** is a 3-dimensional shape that looks like a box. To find the volume of a rectangular prism, you do not need to count all of the cubes that fill it. The following example shows a shortcut method for finding the volume.

EXAMPLE Find the volume of this rectangular prism.

Each cube is 1 cubic inch.

The top layer has 12 cubes. We cannot see all of the middle layer and bottom layer. But each of these layers also has 12 cubes.

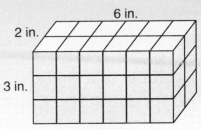

There are 3 layers of cubes. Each layer has 12 cubes. So there are 3 × 12, or 36 cubes in all.

The volume is 36 cubic inches.

Summary: To find the volume of a rectangular prism:

1. Count the number of cubes in one layer.

2. Count the number of layers of cubes.

3. Multiply:
   (number of layers) × (number of cubes in 1 layer)

CHECK YOUR UNDERSTANDING

1. Which volume is larger, 1 cubic yard or 1 cubic meter?

2. Find the volume of each stack of cubes.

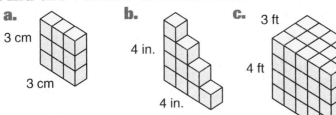

a.
3 cm
3 cm

b.
4 in.
4 in.

c.
3 ft
5 ft
4 ft

Check your answers on page 297.

Capacity

Sometimes we need to know amounts of things that can be poured. All liquids can be poured. Some solids, such as sand and sugar, can be poured, too.

The volume of a container that holds liquids is often called its **capacity.** Capacity is usually measured in such units as **gallons, quarts, pints, cups, fluid ounces, liters,** and **milliliters.**

Liters and milliliters are **metric units.** Gallons, quarts, pints, cups, and fluid ounces are **U.S. customary units.** Most labels for liquid containers give capacity in both metric and U.S. customary units.

The table below shows how different units of capacity compare to each other.

Metric Units

1 liter (L) = 1,000 milliliters (mL)

1 milliliter = $\frac{1}{1,000}$ liter

U.S. Customary Units

1 gallon (gal) = 4 quarts (qt)

1 gallon = 2 half-gallons

1 half-gallon = 2 quarts

1 quart = 2 pints (pt)

1 pint = 2 cups (c)

1 cup = 8 fluid ounces (fl oz)

1 pint = 16 fluid ounces

1 quart = 32 fluid ounces

1 half-gallon = 64 fluid ounces

1 gallon = 128 fluid ounces

You can use the table to change to other units.

EXAMPLE Change 3 quarts to pints, cups, and gallons.

1 quart equals 2 pints. So 3 quarts is 3 × 2, or 6 pints

1 quart equals 2 pints, and each pint equals 2 cups.
So 1 quart equals 4 cups, and 3 quarts is 3 × 4, or 12 cups.

4 quarts equals 1 gallon. So 1 quart equals $\frac{1}{4}$ gallon, and 3 quarts is $\frac{3}{4}$ gallon.

$$3 \text{ qt} = 6 \text{ pt} = \frac{3}{4} \text{ gal}$$

One liter is a little more than 1 quart.

EXAMPLE About how many cups is 2 liters?

1 liter is about 1 quart. 2 liters is about 2 quarts.
Since 1 quart equals 4 cups, 2 quarts is 2 × 4, or 8 cups.

So 2 liters is about 8 cups.

A 2-liter bottle of water contains about how many fluid ounces?

The table shows that 1 cup equals 8 fluid ounces.
So 8 cups is 8 × 8, or 64 fluid ounces.

A 2-liter bottle contains about 64 fluid ounces.

CHECK YOUR UNDERSTANDING

Copy and complete.

1. a. 6 pt = _?_ c **b.** 6 pt = _?_ qt **c.** 12 qt = _?_ gal

2. 10 liters is about how many cups?

3. Which is larger, 1 quart or 40 fluid ounces?

Check your answers on page 297.

Weight

Today, in the United States, we use two different sets of standard units to measure weight.

- The standard unit for weight in the metric system is the **gram.** A small, plastic base-10 cube weighs about 1 gram. Heavier weights are measured in **kilograms.** One kilogram equals 1,000 grams.

- Two standard units for weight in the U.S. customary system are the **ounce** and the **pound.** Heavier weights are measured in pounds. One pound equals 16 ounces. Some weights are reported in both pounds and ounces. For example, we might say that "the box weighs 4 pounds 3 ounces."

The table below lists the units of weight most often used. It shows how these units compare to each other.

Metric Units

1 gram (g) = 1,000 milligrams (mg)	1 metric ton (t) = 1,000 kilograms
1 milligram = $\frac{1}{1,000}$ gram	1 kilogram = $\frac{1}{1,000}$ metric ton
1 kilogram (kg) = 1,000 grams	
1 gram = $\frac{1}{1,000}$ kilogram	

U.S. Customary Units

1 pound (lb) = 16 ounces (oz)	1 ton (T) = 2,000 pounds
1 ounce = $\frac{1}{16}$ pound	1 pound = $\frac{1}{2,000}$ ton

EXAMPLE Arthur's bowling ball weighs 10 pounds 5 ounces. How many ounces does the ball weigh?

One pound equals 16 ounces. So 10 pounds is 10 × 16, or 160 ounces.

10 pounds 5 ounces is 160 + 5, or 165 ounces.

How can we compare two weights, such as 6 ounces and 280 grams, that use different units? One weight uses U.S. customary units, and the other weight uses metric units.

Use the items shown below to compare 1 gram and 1 ounce and to compare 1 pound and 1 kilogram.

small, plastic base-10 cube	30 base-10 cubes	1 pint of strawberries	$2\frac{1}{4}$ pints of strawberries
about 1 gram	about 1 ounce	about 1 pound	about 1 kilogram

EXAMPLE A volleyball weighs 280 grams. A softball weighs 6 ounces. Which ball weighs more?

One ounce equals about 30 grams. So 6 ounces is about 6 × 30, or 180 grams. The softball weighs about 180 grams.

So the volleyball weighs more than the softball.

CHECK YOUR UNDERSTANDING

Is 600 grams heavier than 1 pound?

Check your answer on page 297.

The following pages show samples of different kinds of scales. The **capacity** and the **precision** are given for each scale.

The **capacity** of a scale is the greatest weight that the scale can hold. For example, most infant scales have a capacity of about 25 pounds. An infant scale would not be used to weigh a third grader.

The **precision** of a scale is the accuracy of the scale. If you can read a weight on an infant scale to the nearest ounce, then the precision for that scale is 1 ounce. With a balance scale, you can measure weight to the nearest gram. A balance scale is much more precise than an infant scale because a gram is much lighter than an ounce.

Some scales are extremely precise. They can weigh things that cannot be seen with the naked eye. Other scales are very large. They can be used to weigh objects that can weigh as much as 100 tons (200,000 pounds). Most scales display weights in both metric and U.S. customary units.

CHECK YOUR UNDERSTANDING

1. Arrange the weights from lightest to heaviest:

   1 pound   1 gram   1 kilogram   1 ounce

2. Copy and complete.

   a. _?_ lb = 16 oz

   b. 1,000 mg = _?_ g

   c. 1 kg = _?_ g

   d. 600 g = _?_ kg

   e. 10 lb = _?_ oz

   f. 8,000 lb = _?_ T

   Check your answers on page 297.

Samples of Scales

Types of scales will vary in capacity and precision.

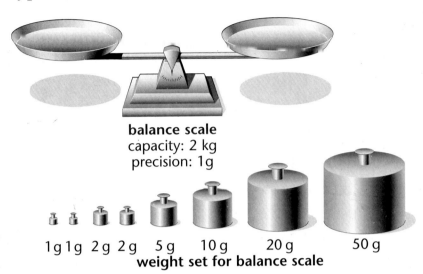

balance scale
capacity: 2 kg
precision: 1 g

1 g 1 g 2 g 2 g 5 g 10 g 20 g 50 g
weight set for balance scale

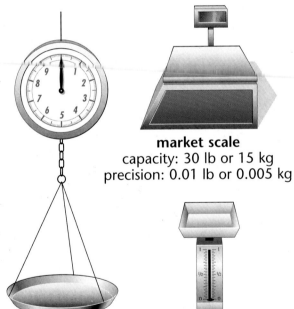

produce scale
capacity: 10 lb
precision: 1 oz

market scale
capacity: 30 lb or 15 kg
precision: 0.01 lb or 0.005 kg

diet/food scales
capacity: 16 oz   capacity: 12 lb or 5 kg
precision: $\frac{1}{2}$ oz   precision: 1 oz or 25 g

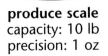

letter scale
capacity: 2 lb
precision: 1 oz

package scale
capacity: 70 lb
precision: 1 lb

platform scale
capacity: 1 T to 1,000 T
precision: 20 lb

bath scale
capacity: 300 lb or 135 kg
precision: 0.1 lb or 50 g

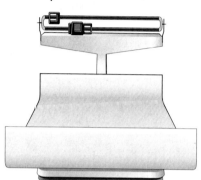

infant scale
capacity: 25 lb
precision: 1 oz

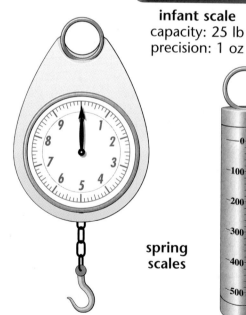

doctor's scale
capacity: 350 lb
precision: $\frac{1}{4}$ lb; 4 oz

spring scales

capacity: 10 oz or 300 g
precision: $\frac{1}{8}$ oz or 5 g

capacity: 18 oz or 500 g
precision: $\frac{1}{2}$ oz or 20 g

Measuring Angles

The Babylonians lived about 3,000 years ago in what is now the country of Iraq. The way we measure angles was invented by the Babylonians. They counted a year as having 360 days. They used this same number, 360, for measuring angles. The angle measurer shown below is their invention.

The circle is divided into 360 equal parts called **degrees.** The numbers printed in the circle are written with a small raised circle (°). The small circle is a symbol for the word *degree.* For example, we read 270° as "270 degrees."

0°
360°
315°
45°
270°
O
90°
225°
135°
180°

Think of walking around the circle. Start at the 0° mark. Walk clockwise around the circle. The degree numbers written in the circle show how many marks on the circle you travel past.

EXAMPLE   When you walk from 0° to 45°, you pass 45 marks along the circle.

When you walk from 0° to 180°, you pass 180 marks. You pass half of the 360 marks on the circle. You are half-way around the circle.

When you walk from 0° to 360°, you pass all 360 marks. You are back where you started.

Here is how to use an angle measurer (protractor) to measure angles.

1. Place the hole in the center of the measurer over the vertex of the angle. The vertex is the point where the sides of the angle meet.

2. Line up the 0° mark on the measurer with the side of the angle where the arrow begins.

3. Find where the other side of the angle crosses the measurer. Read the degree measure.

EXAMPLE

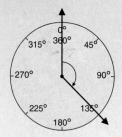

The angle measures 135°.

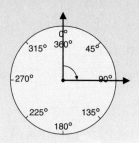

The angle measures 90°.
A 90° angle is $\frac{1}{4}$ turn on the circle.
A 90° angle is called a **right angle**.

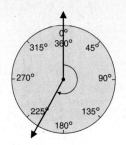

The angle measures between 180° and 225°.

The angle measure is closer to 225° than it is to 180°.

Reference Frames

Temperature

The **temperature** of something is how hot or cold it is. A **thermometer** measures temperature. The common thermometer is a glass tube that contains a liquid. When the temperature goes up, the liquid expands and moves up the tube. When the temperature goes down, the liquid shrinks and moves down the tube.

In the U.S. customary system, temperature is measured in **degrees Fahrenheit (°F).** In the metric system, temperature is measured in **degrees Celsius (°C).**

EXAMPLES   Water freezes at 32°F or 0°C. Water boils at 212°F or 100°C.

A small thermometer for taking body temperatures usually has marks that are spaced $\frac{2}{10}$ (0.2) of a degree apart. This allows you to make very accurate measurements of body temperature.

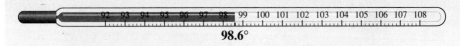

98.6°

Normal body temperature is about 98.6°F.

Temperatures may be negative numbers. The temperature –20°F is read as "negative 20 degrees," or as "20 degrees below 0."

Most thermometers have marks that are spaced
2 degrees apart.

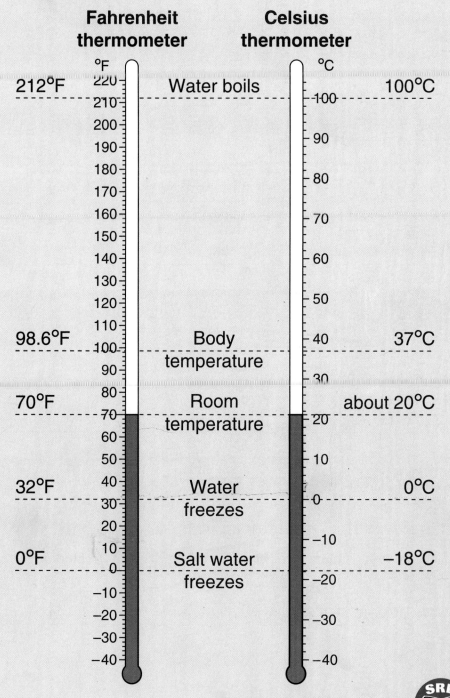

Fahrenheit thermometer

Celsius thermometer

212°F — Water boils — 100°C

98.6°F — Body temperature — 37°C

70°F — Room temperature — about 20°C

32°F — Water freezes — 0°C

0°F — Salt water freezes — −18°C

Sometimes you want to find the difference between two temperatures. Sometimes the temperature may change, and you want to find the new temperature.

EXAMPLE Find the temperature difference between 48°F and 94°F.

One way to find the difference is to start with the smaller number and count up to the larger number.
Start with 48. Add 2 to get 50. Then add 40 to get 90. Then add 4 to get 94. The total added is 2 + 40 + 4, or 46.

Another way to find the difference is to subtract.
94 − 48 = 46.

The difference is 46 degrees, or 46°F.

EXAMPLE Find the temperature difference between 52°C and −20°C.

Start with the negative temperature, −20°C. Add 20° to get 0°C. Then add 52° to get 52°C. The total added is 72°.

The difference is 72°.

EXAMPLE The temperature was 40°F at 6:00. By 9:00 the temperature had gone down 30 degrees. What was the temperature at 9:00?

Since the temperature went down, subtract 30° from the starting temperature. 40 − 30 = 10.

The temperature was 10°F at 9:00.

CHECK YOUR UNDERSTANDING

1. Find the missing temperatures.

	Fahrenheit degrees (°F)	Celsius degrees (°C)
a. Water boils	212°F	_?_ °C
b. Water freezes	_?_ °F	0°C
c. Body temperature	_?_ °F	37°C
d. Room temperature	70°F	_?_ °C
e. Salt water freezes	0°F	_?_ °C

2. Find the temperature difference between 15°F and 41°F.

3. Find the temperature difference between −10°C and 70°C.

4. The temperature was 73°F at noon. By 4:00 P.M. the temperature had fallen 35°F. What was the temperature at 4:00 P.M.?

Check your answers on page 297.

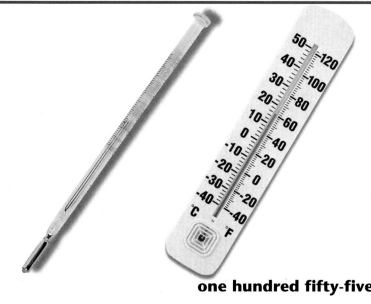

Time

We use **time** in two ways:
1. To tell when something happens.
2. To tell how long something takes or lasts.

> **EXAMPLE** Marta goes to sleep at 9:30 P.M. She
> wakes up at 7:15 A.M. Marta has slept for 9 hours
> and 45 minutes.
>
> 9:30 P.M. and 7:15 A.M. are times that tell when
> something happens. 9 hours and 45 minutes tells
> how long Marta's sleep lasted.

A.M. is an abbreviation that means "before noon." It
refers to the period from midnight to noon. P.M. is an
abbreviation that means "after noon." It refers to the
period from noon to midnight. Noon is written as
12:00 P.M. Midnight is written as 12:00 A.M.

The table below shows how units of time compare.

Units of Time		
1 minute	=	60 seconds
1 hour	=	60 minutes
1 day	=	24 hours
1 week	=	7 days
1 month	=	28, 29, 30, or 31 days
1 year	=	12 months
1 year	=	52 weeks plus 1 day, or
		52 weeks plus 2 days (in leap year)
1 year	=	365 days, or 366 days (in leap year)
1 decade	=	10 years
1 century	=	100 years
1 millennium	=	1,000 years

One second is a very short time. But we often want to measure times to a fraction of a second. Many wristwatches have a stopwatch that records times to the nearest $\frac{1}{100}$ (or 0.01) second.

EXAMPLE Running events in the Olympics are timed to the nearest 0.01 second. In the 1988 Olympics, Florence Griffith-Joyner won the 100-meter run. Her time was 10.54 seconds.

CHECK YOUR UNDERSTANDING

1. What do A.M. and P.M. stand for?

2. Put these times in order:

7:30 P.M. 12:00 A.M. 12:00 P.M. 4:15 A.M.

9:45 P.M. 10:50 A.M. 3:05 P.M. 2:55 A.M.

3. How many years in 1 decade?

4. How many years in 3 centuries?

Copy and complete.

5. 1 day = __?__ hours **6.** 4 weeks = __?__ days

7. **Challenge:** How many seconds in 1 hour?

Check your answers on page 297.

Calendars

The Earth revolves around the sun. It takes 365 days, 5 hours, 48 minutes, and 46 seconds to make one complete revolution. This time is the exact meaning of one year.

We use a **calendar** to keep track of the days of each week and month in a year. The calendars for most years show 365 days. But every four years, we add an extra day in February. These special years are called **leap years.** Each leap year has 366 days.

Years that are leap years follow a pattern. The pattern has two rules:

1. Any year that can be divided by 4 (with no remainder) is a leap year. So 2004, 2008, and 2012 are all leap years.

2. Years that end in 00 are special cases. They are leap years only when they can be divided by 400 (with no remainder). So 2000 and 2400 are leap years. But 1900 and 2100 are *not* leap years.

Here is a list of the months of the year. It shows the number of days in each month.

January	31 days	July	31 days
February	28 or 29* days	August	31 days
March	31 days	September	30 days
April	30 days	October	31 days
May	31 days	November	30 days
June	30 days	December	31 days

* 29 days in leap year

Here is a calendar for the year 2000. This was a leap year.

2000

JANUARY						
S	M	T	W	T	F	S
						1
2	3	4	5	6	7	8
9	10	11	12	13	14	15
16	17	18	19	20	21	22
23	24	25	26	27	28	29
30	31					

FEBRUARY						
		1	2	3	4	5
6	7	8	9	10	11	12
13	14	15	16	17	18	19
20	21	22	23	24	25	26
27	28	29				

MARCH						
		1	2	3	4	
5	6	7	8	9	10	11
12	13	14	15	16	17	18
19	20	21	22	23	24	25
26	27	28	29	30	31	

APRIL						
						1
2	3	4	5	6	7	8
9	10	11	12	13	14	15
16	17	18	19	20	21	22
23	24	25	26	27	28	29
30						

MAY						
S	M	T	W	T	F	S
	1	2	3	4	5	6
7	8	9	10	11	12	13
14	15	16	17	18	19	20
21	22	23	24	25	26	27
28	29	30	31			

JUNE						
				1	2	3
4	5	6	7	8	9	10
11	12	13	14	15	16	17
18	19	20	21	22	23	24
25	26	27	28	29	30	

JULY						
						1
2	3	4	5	6	7	8
9	10	11	12	13	14	15
16	17	18	19	20	21	22
23	24	25	26	27	28	29
30	31					

AUGUST						
		1	2	3	4	5
6	7	8	9	10	11	12
13	14	15	16	17	18	19
20	21	22	23	24	25	26
27	28	29	30	31		

SEPTEMBER						
S	M	T	W	T	F	S
					1	2
3	4	5	6	7	8	9
10	11	12	13	14	15	16
17	18	19	20	21	22	23
24	25	26	27	28	29	30

OCTOBER						
1	2	3	4	5	6	7
8	9	10	11	12	13	14
15	16	17	18	19	20	21
22	23	24	25	26	27	28
29	30	31				

NOVEMBER						
		1	2	3	4	
5	6	7	8	9	10	11
12	13	14	15	16	17	18
19	20	21	22	23	24	25
26	27	28	29	30		

DECEMBER						
					1	2
3	4	5	6	7	8	9
10	11	12	13	14	15	16
17	18	19	20	21	22	23
24	25	26	27	28	29	30
31						

EXAMPLES Thanksgiving is always on the 4th Thursday in November. So Thanksgiving was November 23rd in 2000.

January 1, 2000 was a Saturday. So the last day of 1999 (December 31, 1999) was a Friday.

CHECK YOUR UNDERSTANDING

1. Which months have 30 days?

2. What day of the week is January 1, 2001?

3. What date does the 4th Monday of May fall on?

4. What is the day of the week and the date one week after July 28?

Check your answers on page 297.

Seasons and Length of Day

The year is divided into four **seasons.**

Dates	Season North of Equator	Season South of Equator
Dec 22 to Mar 20	Winter	Summer
Mar 21 to Jun 20	Spring	Fall
Jun 21 to Sep 21	Summer	Winter
Sep 22 to Dec 21	Fall	Spring

On March 21 and September 22, day and night have the same length. They are each 12 hours long at every place on Earth.

The first day of winter is the shortest day and longest night of the year. This is December 22 in the United States. The first day of winter is June 21 for any place south of the equator.

The first day of summer is the longest day and shortest night of the year. This is June 21 in the United States. The first day of summer is December 22 for any place south of the equator.

The length of a day is the time from sunrise to sunset. The length of day in most places is always changing. For half of the year, each day is longer than the day before. And for the other half of the year, each day is shorter than the day before.

The length of a day depends upon the time of year (the date). It also depends upon how far you are from the equator. The table below shows the length of day at some different places.

Length of Day (in hours and minutes)

Date	Equator	Houston, Texas	Seward, Alaska	North Pole
March 21	12 hr 0 min	12 hr 0 min	12 hr 0 min	12 hr 0 min
June 21	12 hr 0 min	14 hr 4 min	18 hr 49 min	24 hr 0 min
September 22	12 hr 0 min	12 hr 0 min	12 hr 0 min	12 hr 0 min
December 22	12 hr 0 min	10 hr 14 min	5 hr 54 min	0 hr 0 min

On March 21, all places have day and night of equal length. On September 22, all places have day and night of equal length.

EXAMPLE Compare Houston and Seward on June 21. Both cities are north of the equator, so June 21 is the first day of summer in both places. It is also the longest day of the year. Seward is much farther from the equator than Houston is. And Seward gets about 5 more hours of sunlight than Houston on June 21.

CHECK YOUR UNDERSTANDING

1. What are the beginning and ending dates for spring in the place where you live?

2. Compare Houston and Seward on December 22.

Check your answers on page 298.

one hundred sixty-one SRB 161

Coordinate Grids

Sometimes we use two number lines to make a **coordinate grid.**

We locate points on the coordinate grid with two numbers. The numbers are written in parentheses.

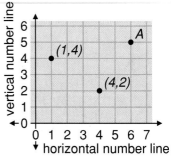

EXAMPLE   Locate the point (4,2) on the coordinate grid.

Start at the point marked with 0 on the horizontal number line. Move along the horizontal number line to the point marked 4. Then move up from there to the line that is named 2 on the vertical number line.

The point where you stop is named (4,2).

EXAMPLE   Name the location of point *A.*

Find the number on the horizontal number line that is directly under point *A.* That number is 6. Then find the number on the vertical number line that is directly to the left of point *A.* That number is 5.

The name for point A is (6,5).

Pairs of numbers like (6,5) and (1,4) are called **ordered pairs.**

The numbers in parentheses are called the **coordinates** of the point. The numbers 6 and 5 are the coordinates of the point (6,5).

CHECK YOUR UNDERSTANDING

1. Which letter names the
point at each location?
   a. (4,1)   **b.** (3,5)

2. Write the location of
each point.
   a. point *C*   **b.** point *R*

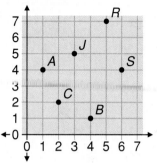

3. Use the coordinate grid on
the map to write the coordinates for each place.

Campground Map

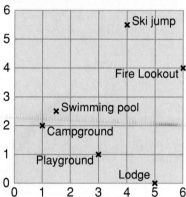

a. Campground   (1,2)

b. Fire Lookout   (___,___)

c. Lodge   (___,___)

d. Playground   (___,___)

e. Ski Jump   (___,$5\frac{1}{2}$)

f. Swimming pool (___,___)

Check your answers on page 298.

Scale Drawings

Maps and drawings often have a **distance key.**
The distance key tells how to change the distances
on a map or drawing to real-life distances.
Sometimes the distance key is called a **scale.**

EXAMPLE Josh used grid paper to draw a map.
The distance key on Josh's map shows that every
1 inch on his map equals 100 feet of real distance.

Josh walks from home to school by going along Main Street and then
along Ellis Avenue. On his map it is 1 inch from his house to Ellis
Avenue. And it is another 3 inches along Ellis Avenue to the school.
The total distance from Josh's house to school is 4 inches. Each inch
equals 100 feet. So the school is 400 feet from Josh's house.

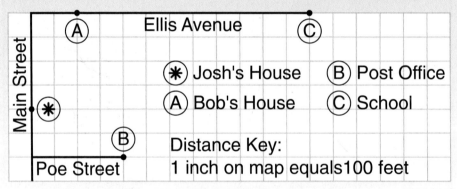

The grid paper Josh used has 4 grid squares per inch. So every grid
square is $\frac{1}{4}$-inch long and stands for 25 feet of real distance.
Bob's house is 6 grid squares away from Josh's house.
So Bob's house is 6 × 25, or 150 feet away from Josh's house.

Estimation

When You Have to Estimate

An **estimate** is an answer that is close to an exact answer. You make estimates every day.

- You estimate how long it will take to drive from one place to another.

- You estimate how much money you will need to buy some things at the store.

- You estimate how many inches you will grow in the next year.

It may be impossible to find an exact answer. When this happens, you *must* estimate the answer.

EXAMPLE Weather forecasters predict temperatures for the next day. They must estimate because they don't know what the exact temperatures will be.

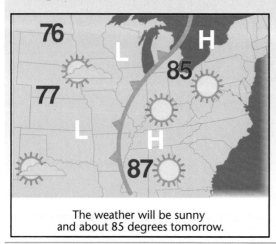

76
L   H
85
77
L   H
87

The weather will be sunny
and about 85 degrees tomorrow.

They use words like **expect, predict,** and **about.** These words let people know that they are giving estimates, not exact amounts.

Ballpark Estimates

Sometimes you do not need to find an exact answer. A good estimate, called a **ballpark estimate,** is a close answer that helps you answer a question.

EXAMPLE   Bea has $5.00. Is that enough money to buy a $1.39 bottle of juice and a $2.89 pizza?

Bea can estimate. She can use simple numbers that are close to the real prices.

	Exact Prices	Simple Numbers That are Close
$2.89 is almost $3.	$2.89	$3.00
$1.39 is almost $1.50.	$1.39	+ $1.50
$3 + $1.50 equals $4.50.		$4.50

Bea has enough money to buy the juice and the pizza.

EXAMPLE   Ali read 12 pages in half an hour. About how long will it take him to read 33 pages?

Estimate how long it will take Ali. Use simple numbers that are close to the exact numbers.

	Exact Numbers	Simple Numbers That are Close
12 is close to 10	12 pages	10 pages
33 is close to 30	33 pages	30 pages

Reading 30 pages should take about 3 times as long as reading 10 pages.

It will take Ali about $1\frac{1}{2}$ hours to read 33 pages.

Estimate to Check Calculations

Sometimes you do want an exact answer. Making an estimate can help you check your answer. Your estimate should be close to the exact answer. If your estimate is not close, you know that you should try the calculation again.

EXAMPLE Amit took a trip. On Monday he went 526 miles. On Tuesday he went 348 miles. On Wednesday he went 482 miles. Amit added the three numbers and got 982.

Amit made a ballpark estimate to check his answer. He used simple numbers that were close to the numbers in the problem.

	Exact Numbers	Simple Numbers That are Close
526 is close to 500.	526	500
348 is close to 300.	348	300
482 is close to 500.	482	+ 500
Add the 3 simple numbers.		1,300

Amit knows that his answer of 982 must be wrong. He added the three numbers again. This time he got 1,356.

The new answer makes more sense. It is close to his estimate of 1,300.

Adjusting Numbers

Try to use simple numbers when you estimate.
The simple numbers should be close to the exact
numbers in the problem.

Here is one way to **adjust** a number and get a
simpler number.

1. Keep the first digit of the number.

2. Replace the other digits of the number by zeros.

EXAMPLES

Exact Number	Adjusted Number
147	100
92	90
4,600	4,000
128,720	100,000
4	4

EXAMPLES Each problem below is written again
using adjusted numbers. The adjusted numbers are
used to find an estimate. The estimates are circled.

Exact Numbers	Adjusted Numbers		Exact Numbers	Adjusted Numbers
347	300		452	400
− 212	− 200		+ 86	+ 80
	(100)			(480)

A more accurate way to adjust numbers is to round the numbers. Here is a way to round a number:

EXAMPLES	Round 47	Round 632
Step 1 Write the number you are rounding.	47	632
Step 2 Keep the first digit. Replace the other digits by zeros. This is the lower number.	40	600
Step 3 Add 1 to the first digit. This is the higher number.	50	700
Step 4 Is the number you are rounding closer to the lower number or the higher number?	higher	lower
Step 5 Round to the closer of the two numbers.	50	600

Sometimes the number you are rounding is halfway between the lower number and higher number. When this happens, round to the higher number.

EXAMPLE You are rounding 85.

The lower number is 80. The higher number is 90. 85 is halfway between 80 and 90.

So round 85 to 90, which is the higher number.

CHECK YOUR UNDERSTANDING
Round each number.

1. 59   **2.** 14   **3.** 45   **4.** 555   **5.** 6,401

6. Estimate the sum 282 + 47 by using rounded numbers.

Check your answers on page 298.

Patterns & Functions

Picture Patterns

Shapes are often arranged in regular ways to form patterns. Floor and ceiling tiles often form a pattern.

The pictures below show some different ways that bricks are used to build walls. Each way of laying bricks forms a different pattern.

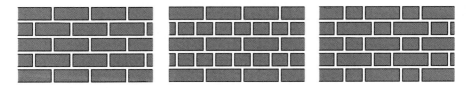

Sometimes a picture pattern is given. You are asked to continue the pattern. You must decide what the next shape in the pattern will be.

To find the next shape for a pattern, you will have to guess. Your guess should be a good guess, not a wild guess. Look carefully at what is given and try to find a pattern. Use the pattern to help guess what the next shape will be.

EXAMPLE What is the next shape in this picture pattern?

The picture shows a series of squares. Each square contains one dot. The dot moves clockwise from one corner to the next.

So the next shape will look like this:

Here are some other picture patterns. There is enough information in the picture to make a good guess about the next shape.

EXAMPLE Find the next shape in this picture pattern:

 ?

Each shape in the series has a small circle.
The number of arrows increases by one each time.

So the next shape will have 5 arrows.

EXAMPLE Find the next shape in this picture pattern:

 ?

Each shape has two parts. One part is a polygon. Each polygon in the series has one more side than the polygon before it. The last shape is a pentagon (5 sides). So the next shape will be a hexagon (6 sides).

The other part is a set of dots inside the polygon. Each polygon has one more dot than the polygon before it. The pentagon has 3 dots. So the next shape will have 4 dots.

The next shape for this picture pattern is

CHECK YOUR UNDERSTANDING

Draw the next shape in each picture pattern.

1. ▷ △ ⬠   **2.** •   •• 　 •••
　　　　　　　　　　　　　　　　　　 • 　•••

Check your answers on page 298.

Number Patterns

Dot pictures can be used to represent numbers.
The dot pictures can help us find number patterns.

Even numbers

2   4   6   8   10   12

All numbers that can be divided by 2 (with no
remainder) are called **even numbers.** The dot
picture for an even number has 2 rows. Each row
has the same number of dots.

Odd numbers

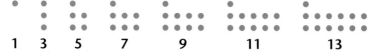

1   3   5   7   9   11   13

All numbers that have a remainder of 1 when they
are divided by 2 are called **odd numbers.** The dot
picture for an odd number has 2 equal rows plus
1 extra dot.

Triangular numbers

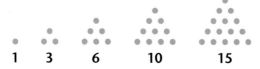

1   3   6   10   15

The dot pictures above are triangles with the same
number of dots on each side. Any number that has a
dot picture like this is called a **triangular number.**

Square numbers

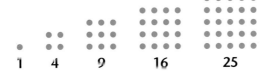

When a number is multiplied by itself, the product is called a **square number.** $3 \times 3 = 9$, so 9 is a square number. $4 \times 4 = 16$, so 16 is a square number. The dot picture for a square number is a square.

Rectangular numbers

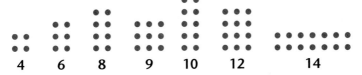

A number is a **rectangular number** if it has a dot picture that forms a rectangle. Each row of the dot picture has the same number of dots. A rectangular number is always the product of two smaller numbers. For example, $12 = 4 \times 3$.

Prime numbers

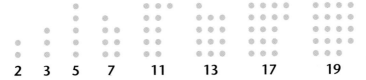

A **prime number** is a number greater than 1 that cannot be divided (with no remainder) by any number other than 1 and itself. This means that prime numbers cannot be fit into rectangular shapes that have 2 or more rows and 2 or more columns.

one hundred seventy-five $\overset{\text{SRB}}{175}$

Frames and Arrows

A Frames-and-Arrows diagram is one way to show a number pattern. This type of diagram has three parts.

- A set of **frames** that contain numbers.
- **Arrows** that show the path from one frame to the next frame.
- A box with an arrow below it. The box has a **rule** written inside. The rule tells how to change the number in one frame to get the number in the next frame.

EXAMPLE Here is a Frames-and-Arrows diagram.

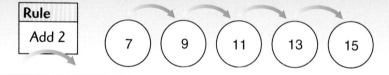

EXAMPLE Use the rule to fill in the empty frames.

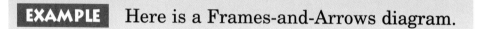
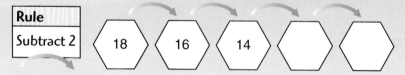

The rule is "Subtract 2." Look at the frame with the number 14. If you subtract 2 from 14, the result is 12. Write 12 in the next frame. Then subtract 2 from 12. The result is 10. Write 10 in the last frame. The filled in diagram looks like this.

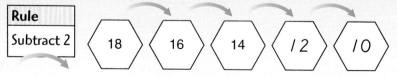

Sometimes the rule is not given. You must use the numbers in the frames to find the rule.

EXAMPLE Find the rule for this diagram.

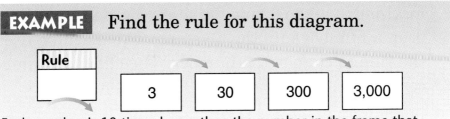

Each number is 10 times larger than the number in the frame that comes before it.

So the rule is "Multiply by 10," or "× 10."

Sometimes the rule is not given and the frames are not all filled in. Find the rule first. Then use the rule to fill in the empty frames.

EXAMPLE Find the rule and fill in the empty frames.

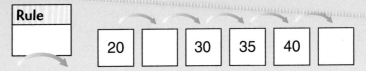

The numbers 30, 35, and 40 can help you to find the rule. Each number is 5 more than the number in the frame before it.

So the rule is "Add 5."

Now use the rule to fill in the empty frames. The second frame contains the number 20 + 5, or 25. The last frame contains the number 40 + 5, or 45.

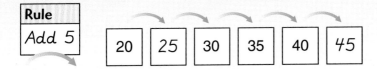

SRB

Function Machines

A **function machine** is an imaginary machine. The machine is given a rule for changing numbers. You drop a number into the machine. The machine uses the rule to change the number. The changed number comes out of the machine.

Here is a picture of a function machine. The machine has been given the rule "+3." The machine will add 3 to any number that is put into it.

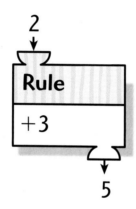

EXAMPLES If you drop 2 into the function machine above, it will add 2 + 3. The number 5 will come out.

If you drop 1 into the machine, it will add 1 + 3. The number 4 will come out.

If you drop 0 into the machine, it will add 0 + 3. The number 3 will come out.

Function Machines and "What's My Rule?"

You can use a table of In and Out numbers to keep track of the way a function machine changes numbers.

Write the numbers that are put into the machine in the **in** column.

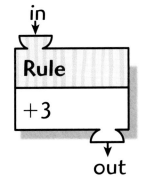

in	out
0	3
1	4
2	5
3	6

Write the numbers that come out of the machine in the **out** column.

EXAMPLE The rule is +10. You know the numbers that are put into the machine. Find the numbers that come out of the machine.

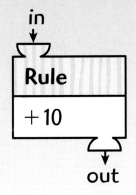

in	out
39	
54	
163	

If 39 is put in, then 49 comes out.
If 54 is put in, then 64 comes out.
If 163 is put in, then 173 comes out.

---

one hundred seventy-nine

EXAMPLE The rule is −6. You know the numbers that come out of the machine. Find the numbers that were put into the machine.

in

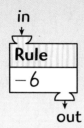

Rule

−6

out

in	out
	20
	0
	10

The machine subtracts 6 from any number that is put into it. The number that comes out is always 6 less than the number put in.

If 20 comes out, then 26 was the number put in.
If 0 comes out, then 6 was the number put in.
If 10 comes out, then 16 was the number put in.

If you have a table of some In and Out numbers, you can find the rule.

EXAMPLE The rule is not known. Use the table to find the rule.

in

Rule

?

out

in	out
55	60
85	90
103	108

Each number in the **out** column is 5 more than the number in the **in** column.

The rule is Add 5 or +5.

Problem Solving

Solving Number Stories

Solving problems is a big part of mathematics. Good problem solvers often follow a few simple steps every time they solve a problem. When you are trying to solve a problem, you can follow these same steps.

A Guide to Solving Number Stories

1. What do you know from reading the story?

2. What do you want to find out?

3. What will you do? Do it. Record what you did.

4. Answer the question. If you can, write a number model to show what you did.

5. Check. Ask, "Does my answer make sense? How do I know?"

These steps can take a lot of work.

1. What do you know from reading the story?
   - Read the story aloud.
   - Retell the story in your own words.
   - Can you draw a picture or diagram?

2. What do you want to find out?
   - Ask the question in your own words.
   - Is the answer a number?
   - Is the answer a length or other measurement?
   - Can you estimate what the answer would be?

3. What will you do?

- Sometimes it's easy to know how to solve a problem.
- Other times you need to be creative.
- Is the problem like one you have solved before?
- Is there a pattern that you can use?
- Can you compute to find the answer?
- Can you use counters, base-10 blocks, or some other tool?
- Can you make a table?
- Can you guess the answer and check to see if you're right?

Do it. Record what you did.

- Try to show how you solved the problem.
- Draw a picture.
- Write about what you did.

4. Answer the question.

- What are the units?
- Write a sentence that answers the question in the problem.
- If you can, write a number model that fits the problem.

5. Check.

- Ask, "Does my answer make sense? How do I know?"

- Does your answer agree with other people's answers?

- Estimate the answer. Does your answer agree with your estimate?

CHECK YOUR UNDERSTANDING

1. Laurel had 30 pennies. She put 12 pennies in her bank and gave the other pennies to three friends. How many pennies did each friend get?

2. One side of a rectangle is 30 cm. Another side is 10 cm. What is the perimeter of the rectangle?

3. Delna bought 6 pencils for 72¢. How much did each pencil cost?

4. The product of two numbers is 12. The sum of the numbers is 7. What are the numbers?

5. Ms. Johnson's third grade class has more boys than girls. If there were two more boys, there would be twice as many boys as girls. There are 8 girls in the class. How many boys are there?

Check your answers on page 298.

Guide to Solving Number Stories

1. What do you know?

2. What do you want to find out?

3. What will you do?

- ❥ Draw a picture?
- ❥ Draw a diagram?
- ❥ Make tallies?
- ❥ Add?
- ❥ Subtract?
- ❥ Multiply?
- ❥ Divide?

Do it.

4. Answer the question.

Can you write a number model to show what you did?

5. Check.

Ask: "Does my answer make sense? How do I know?"

Change Number Stories

A number story is a **change story** if an amount is increased or decreased.

If the amount is increased, we call it a **change-to-more** story.

If the amount is decreased, we call it a **change-to-less** story.

EXAMPLE 25 children are riding on a bus. Then 5 more children get on. How many children are on the bus now?

The number of children on the bus has increased. This is a change-to-more number story.

A **change diagram** has spaces to show the **Start, Change,** and **End** numbers in a number story. It can help you solve a change number story.

Start	Change	End
25	+5	?

The change diagram shows the numbers you know and the number you need to find. Add 25 + 5 to solve the problem.

There are 30 children on the bus.

$25 + 5 = 30$ is a **number model** for this number story. The number model shows how the parts of the story are connected.

EXAMPLE A bus leaves school with 35 children on it. At the first stop, 6 children get off. How many children are still on the bus?

Start	Change	End
35	−6	?

The change diagram shows the numbers you know and the number you need to find. You can subtract 35 − 6 to solve the problem.

There are 29 children left on the bus. $35 - 6 = 29$ is a number model for this number story.

EXAMPLE The temperature was 60 degrees at 8:00 A.M. By noon, it was 72 degrees. What was the temperature change?

Start	Change	End
60	?	72

In some change stories, you know the Start and the End. You need to find the Change. Ask yourself, "What do I need to add to 60 to get 72?" The answer is 12.

The temperature increased 12 degrees. $60 + 12 = 72$ is a number model for this number story.

Parts-and-Total Number Stories

A number story is a **parts-and-total story** if two or more parts are combined to form a total. Here are some simple examples of parts-and-total stories:

• Andy earned $8. Derek earned $11. Together they earned $19. The two parts are $8 and $11. The total earnings is $19.

• A math quiz had 20 problems. Paula had 14 correct answers and 6 incorrect answers. The total is 20 answers. The two parts are 14 answers and 6 answers.

EXAMPLE There are 14 boys and 11 girls in Mr. Wilson's class. How many children are in his class?

A **parts-and-total diagram** has spaces to show each **Part** and the **Total** in a number story.

The Parts are known.

You are looking for the Total.

Add 14 + 11 to solve the problem.

Total	
?	
Part	**Part**
14	11

There are 25 children in Mr. Wilson's class. 14 + 11 = 25 is a **number model** for this number story. The number model shows how the different parts of the story are connected.

In some parts-and-total stories, you know the total but not all of the parts. You need to find one of the parts.

> **EXAMPLE** 35 children are riding on a bus. 20 of them are boys. How many girls are riding on the bus?

The Total is known.

And one Part of the Total is known.

You are looking for the other Part.

Total	
35	
Part	**Part**
20	?

One way to solve the problem is to ask yourself, "What do I need to add to 20 to get 35?" The answer is 15.

There are 15 girls on the bus. $20 + 15 = 35$ is one number model for this number story.

Another way to solve the problem is to subtract the number of boys from the total number of children.

$35 - 20 = 15$, so there are 15 girls on the bus. $35 - 20 = 15$ is another number model for this number story.

Comparison Number Stories

In a **comparison story,** two quantities are compared. The **difference** between these quantities tells how much more or less one quantity is than the other.

EXAMPLE   There are 12 third graders and 8 second graders. How many more third graders are there than second graders?

A **comparison diagram** has spaces to show each **Quantity** and the **Difference** in a number story. It can help you solve a comparison number story.

The diagram shows that 2 Quantities are known and you are looking for the Difference.

Quantity
12

Quantity	Difference
8	?

One way to solve the problem is to ask yourself, "What do I add to 8 to get 12?"

There are 4 more third graders. $8 + 4 = 12$ is one **number model** for this number story.

Another way to solve the problem is to subtract the smaller number from the larger number. The difference is $12 - 8$.

The answer is 4. Another number model for this number story is $12 - 8 = 4$.

Diagrams for Equal-Groups Problems

It often helps to fill in a diagram as you solve an equal-groups problem. The diagram has spaces to keep track of three things:

- the number of groups
- the number of objects in each group
- the total number of objects

Fill in the diagram with the numbers you know. Then write a question mark (?) for the number you want to find.

When do you multiply? If the total number of objects is not known, then you multiply to find it.

EXAMPLE There are 4 rows with 6 chairs in each row. How many chairs are there in all?

There are 4 groups of 6.

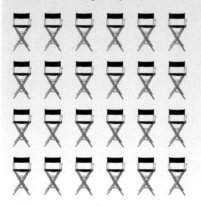

Groups	Objects in each group	Total objects
rows	chairs per row	chairs
4	6	?

To find the total number of chairs, multiply 4 by 6.

$4 \times 6 = 24$ is a number model for this problem.

There are 24 chairs in all.

When do you divide? If the total number of objects is known, then you divide to find the missing number.

EXAMPLE 24 cards are placed in 4 equal piles. How many cards go in each pile?

You know the total number of objects and the number of piles (groups). You need to find the number of objects in each pile.

Divide the total number of cards by the number of piles. Divide 24 by 4.

piles	cards per pile	cards
4	?	24

There are 6 cards in each pile.

$24 \div 4 = 6$ is a number model for this problem.

EXAMPLE Each table must have 6 chairs. There are 33 chairs. How many tables can have 6 chairs?

You know the total number of objects and the number of objects per group. You need to find the number of groups.

Divide the total number of chairs by the number of chairs in 1 group. Divide 33 by 6.

tables	chairs per table	chairs
?	6	33

Five tables can have 6 chairs. There are 3 chairs left over.

$33 \div 6 = 5$ (remainder 3) is a number model for this problem.

Games

Addition Top-It

Materials □ number cards 0–10 (4 of each)
Players 2 to 4

Directions

1. Shuffle the cards. Place the deck number-side down on the playing surface.

2. Each player turns over two cards and calls out the sum of the numbers.

3. The player with the highest sum wins the round and takes all the cards.

4. In case of a tie for the highest sum, each tied player turns over two more cards and calls out the sum of the two cards. The player with the highest sum then takes all the cards from both plays.

5. The game ends when not enough cards are left for each player to have another turn.

6. The player who has the most cards wins.

EXAMPLE Ann turns over a 6 and a 7. She calls out 13. Joe turns over a 10 and a 4. He calls out 14. Joe has the higher sum. He takes all 4 cards.

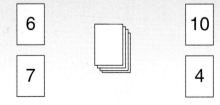

Angle Race

Materials   ☐ 24-pin circular geoboard, or Circular
Geoboard Paper (*Math Masters,* p. 103)

☐ rubber bands, or straightedge and
pencil

☐ set of degree-measure cards (*Math
Masters,* p. 102)

Players   2

Directions

1. Shuffle the cards. Place them facedown.

2. If you have a circular geoboard, stretch a rubber
band from the center peg to the 0° peg. If you
do *not* have a circular geoboard, use circular
geoboard paper. Draw a line segment from the
center dot to the 0° dot. Instead of stretching
rubber bands, you will draw line segments.

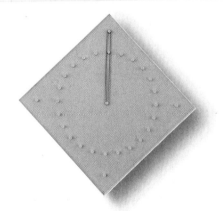
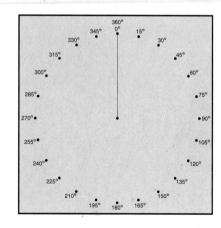

Take turns. On your turn:

3. Select the top card.

4. Make an angle on the geoboard that has the same degree measure as shown on the card. Use the last rubber band you put on the geoboard as one side of your angle. Make the second side of your angle by stretching another rubber band from the center peg to a peg on the circle, going clockwise.

5. Rubber bands may not go past the 360° (or 0°) peg. If you can't make an angle without going past the 360° peg, you lose your turn.

6. The first player to complete an angle exactly on the 360° peg wins.

EXAMPLE   The first player draws a 30° card. The player makes a 30° angle by stretching a rubber band from the center peg to the 30° peg. The second player draws a 75° card. This player makes a 75° angle by stretching a rubber band from the center peg to the 105° peg—and so forth, around the circle.

Array Bingo

Materials ☐ *Array Bingo* cards (*Math Masters*, p. 146)

☐ number cards 1–20 (1 of each)

Players   2 or 3

Directions

1. Each player arranges his or her array cards faceup in a 4-by-4 array.

2. Shuffle the number cards. Place them facedown.

3. Players take turns. When it is your turn, draw a number card. Look for an array card with that number of dots and turn it facedown. If there is no matching array card, your turn ends.

4. The first player to turn a card facedown so that a row, column, or diagonal of cards is all facedown, calls out "Bingo!"

5. If all the number cards are used before someone wins, shuffle the deck and continue playing.

EXAMPLE

Mary draws the number card 4. She turns over the card with the 2 x 2 array and calls out "Bingo."

Baseball Multiplication

Materials ☐ *Baseball Multiplication* Game Mat
(*Math Masters,* p. 50)
☐ 2 six-sided dice
☐ 4 pennies

Players 2 teams of one or more players each

Directions

The rules are similar to the rules for baseball, but this game lasts only 3 innings. In each inning, each team bats until it makes 3 outs. Teams flip a coin to decide who bats first. The team with the most runs when the game is over wins.

Pitching and batting: Members of the team not at bat take turns "pitching." They roll the two dice to get two factors. Players on the "batting" team take turns multiplying the two factors and saying the product.

The pitching team checks the product. (Use a calculator or use the Multiplication/Division Facts Table on page 46.) An incorrect answer is a strike, and another pitch is thrown. Three strikes make an out.

Hits and runs: If the answer is correct, the batter checks the Scoring Chart on the game mat. If the chart shows a hit, the batter moves a penny to a base as shown in the Scoring Chart. Runners already on bases are moved ahead of the batter by the same number of bases. A run is scored every time a runner crosses home plate.

Keeping score: For each inning, keep a tally of runs scored and outs made. Use the Runs-and-Outs Tally on the game mat. At the end of the inning, record the number of runs on the Scoreboard.

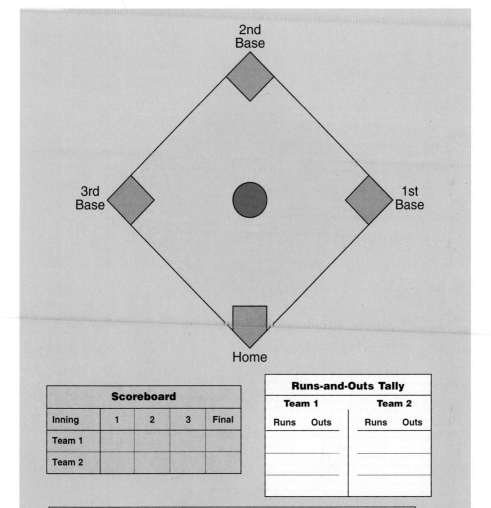

Scoreboard				
Inning	1	2	3	Final
Team 1				
Team 2				

Runs-and-Outs Tally			
Team 1		Team 2	
Runs	Outs	Runs	Outs

Scoring Chart (for two 6-sided dice)	
36 = Home run (score a run)	6 to 15 = Single (go to 1st base)
25 to 35 = Triple (go to 3rd base)	5 or less = Out (record an out)
16 to 24 = Double (go to 2nd base)	

Baseball Multiplication

(Advanced Version)

Materials □ *Baseball Multiplication* Game Mat
(Advanced Version) (*Math Masters*,
p. 51)
□ twelve-sided die
□ 4 pennies

Players 2 teams of one or more players each

Directions

Members of one team take turns "pitching." They
roll the die twice to get two factors. Players on the
"batting" team take turns multiplying the two
factors and giving the product. When a batter gives
the correct product, check the Scoring Chart on the
game mat.

The rest of the game is the same as a regular game
of *Baseball Multiplication.*

You can make the Advanced Version of this game a
little bit easier: If the die comes up as "11" or "12"
on either roll, pretend that the die came up as "10."

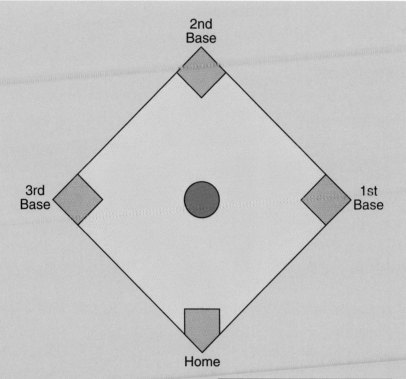

Scoreboard				
Inning	1	2	3	Final
Team 1				
Team 2				

Runs-and-Outs Tally			
Team 1		Team 2	
Runs	Outs	Runs	Outs

Scoring Chart (for 2 rolls of a 12-sided die)	
91 or more = Home run (score a run)	21 to 50 = Single (go to 1st base)
76 to 90 = Triple (go to 3rd base)	20 or less = Out (record an out)
51 to 75 = Double (go to 2nd base)	

Beat the Calculator (Addition)

Materials ☐ number cards 0–9 (4 of each)
           ☐ calculator

Players 3

Directions

1. One player is the "Caller." A second player is the "Calculator." The third player is the "Brain."

2. Shuffle the cards and place them facedown on the table.

3. The Caller draws two cards from the number deck and asks for the sum of the numbers.

4. The Calculator solves the problem with a calculator. The Brain solves it without a calculator. The Caller decides who got the answer first.

5. Players trade roles every 10 turns or so.

EXAMPLE The Caller draws a 2 and a 9. The Caller says, "2 plus 9."

The Brain and the Calculator each solve the problem.

The Caller decides who got the answer first.

Beat the Calculator (Multiplication)

Materials ☐ number cards 1–10 (4 of each)

☐ calculator

Players 3

Directions

1. One player is the "Caller." A second player is the "Calculator." The third player is the "Brain."

2. Shuffle the cards and place them facedown on the table.

3. The Caller draws two cards from the number deck and asks for the product of the numbers.

4. The Calculator solves the problem with a calculator. The Brain solves it without a calculator. The Caller decides who got the answer first.

5. The Caller continues to draw two cards at a time from the number deck and asks for the product of the numbers.

6. Players trade roles every 10 turns or so.

EXAMPLE The Caller draws a 10 and a 7. The Caller says, "10 times 7."

The Brain and the Calculator each solve the problem.

The Caller decides who got the answer first.

The Block-Drawing Game

Materials   ☐ paper bag

☐ 7 blocks (all the same size and shape) in 2 or 3 different colors

Players   3 or more

Directions

1. Choose one player to be the "Director."

2. The Director secretly puts 3, 4, or 5 blocks (not all the same color) into a paper bag. The Director tells the other players *how many blocks* are in the bag, but *not* their colors.

3. The object of the game is for the other players to guess how many blocks of *each color* are in the bag.

4. Players take turns taking one block out of the bag, showing it, and replacing it.

5. After each draw, the Director records the color and keeps a tally on a slate or piece of paper.

6. A player may try to guess the colors of the blocks and the number of blocks of each color at any time.

7. If a player guesses incorrectly, the player is out of the game.

8. The first player to guess correctly wins the game.

EXAMPLE

The Director tells the four other players that there are 5 blocks in the bag.

red / /

yellow / /

green /

Tally after 5 draws

After 5 draws, Player 1 guesses 2 red, 2 yellow, and 1 green. This guess is incorrect. Player 1 is out of the game.

red / / /

yellow / /

green / /

Tally after 7 draws

After 7 draws, Player 2 guesses 2 red, 2 yellow, and 1 green. This guess is incorrect. Player 2 is out of the game.

Player 3 then guesses 3 red, 1 yellow, and 1 green. This guess is correct. Player 3 wins the game.

Broken Calculator

Materials □ a calculator for each player
Players 2 or more

Directions

1. Players pretend that one of the number keys on the calculator is broken.

2. One player says a number.

3. All players then try to display that number on the calculator without using the "broken" key.

EXAMPLE Pretend that the 8 key is "broken." Display the number 18.

Here are several ways to display 18 without using the 8 key:

9 ⊕ 7 ⊕ 2 ⊜   19 ⊖ 1 ⊜   9 ⊗ 2 ⊜   36 ⊘ 2 ⊜

Division Arrays

Materials ☐ number cards 6–18 (1 of each)
                 ☐ regular die
                 ☐ 18 counters

Players 2 to 4

Directions

1. Shuffle the cards. Place the deck number-side down on the playing surface.

2. Take turns. When it is your turn, draw a card and take the number of counters shown on the card. You will use the counters to make an array.

3. Now roll the die. The number on the die is the number of equal rows you must have in the array.

4. Make the array with the counters.

5. Your score is the number of counters in one row. If there are no leftover counters, your score is double the number of counters in one row.

6. Keep track of your scores. The player with the highest total at the end of 5 rounds wins.

EXAMPLE

Number card	Die	Array formed	Leftovers?	Score
10	2		no	10
9	2		yes	4

Equivalent Fractions Game

Materials ☐ deck of 32 Fraction Cards (*Math Journal 2*, Activity Sheets 7 and 8)

Players   2

Directions

1. Mix the Fraction Cards. Put them in a stack, picture side down.

2. Turn the top card over near the stack of cards.

3. Take turns. When it is your turn, turn over the top card from the stack. Try to match this card with a picture-side-up card on the table.

   • If you find a match, take the two matching cards. If there are no cards left picture side up, turn the top card over near the stack.

   • If you cannot find a match, place your card picture side up next to the other cards.

4. The game ends when all cards have been matched. The player with more cards wins.

EXAMPLE   The top card is turned over and put on the table. The picture shows $\frac{4}{6}$.

Player 1 turns over the $\frac{2}{3}$ card. This card matches $\frac{4}{6}$. Player 1 takes both cards. Player 1 turns over the top card and puts it near the stack. It shows $\frac{6}{8}$.

Player 2 turns over the $\frac{0}{4}$ card. There is no match. This card is placed next to $\frac{6}{8}$. It is Player 1's turn.

Equivalent Fractions Game
(Advanced Version)

Materials □ deck of 32 Fraction Cards
(*Math Journal 2,* Activity Sheets 7
and 8)

Players 2

Directions

1. Mix the Fraction Cards. Put them in a stack, picture side down.

2. Take the top card from the stack. Place it on the table with the picture side facing up.

3. Take turns. When it is your turn, take the top card from the stack, **but do not turn it over** (keep the picture side down). Try to match the fraction with one of the picture-side-up cards on the table.

   - If you find a match, turn the card over to see if you matched the cards correctly. If you did, take both cards. If there are no cards left picture side up, turn the top card over.

   - If there is a match but you did not find it, the other player can take the matching cards.

   - If there is no match, place your card next to the other cards, picture side up. Your turn is over.

4. The game ends when all cards have been matched. The player with more cards wins.

Factor Bingo

Materials □ number cards 2–9 (4 of each)
□ *Factor Bingo* Game Mat for each player (*Math Masters*, p. 145)
□ 12 pennies or counters for each player

Players 2 to 4

Directions

1. Fill in your own game mat. Choose any 25 numbers from the numbers 2 through 90.

2. Write one number in each square on your grid. You may use a number only once. Be sure to mix them up; they should not all be in order. To help you keep track of the numbers you use, circle them in the list below the game mat.

3. Shuffle the number cards and place them facedown on the table. Any player can turn over the top card. This top card is the "factor."

4. Players check their grids for a number that has the card number as a factor. Players who have a match cover the number with a counter. Turn over the next top card and continue in the same way.

5. You call out "Bingo!" and win the game if you are the first player to get 5 counters in a row, column, or diagonal. You also win if you get 12 counters anywhere on the game mat.

6. If all the cards are used before someone wins, shuffle the cards again and continue playing.

EXAMPLE A 5-card is turned over. The number 5 is the "factor." Any player may place one counter on a number for which 5 is a factor, such as 10, 15, 20, or 25. A player may place only one counter on the game mat for each card that is turned over.

Sample *Factor Bingo* Game Mat

Choose any of the numbers 2–90. You may use a number only once. To help you keep track of the numbers you use, circle them on the list on your Game Mat page.

	2	3	4	5	6	7	8	9	10
11	12	13	14	15	16	17	18	19	20
21	22	23	24	25	26	27	28	29	30
31	32	33	34	35	36	37	38	39	40
41	42	43	44	45	46	47	48	49	50
51	52	53	54	55	56	57	58	59	60
61	62	63	64	65	66	67	68	69	70
71	72	73	74	75	76	77	78	79	80
81	82	83	84	85	86	87	88	89	90

Fraction Top-It

Materials ☐ deck of 32 Fraction Cards
(*Math Journal 2,* Activity Sheets 7 and 8)

Players 2

Directions

Put the 32 cards in a stack, picture side down. Each player turns over a card from the top of the deck and compare the shaded parts of the cards. The player with the larger fraction shaded takes both cards.

If the shaded parts are equal, the fractions are equivalent. Then each player turns over another card. The player with the larger fraction shaded takes all the cards from both plays.

The game is over when all cards have been taken from the stack. The player with more cards wins.

EXAMPLE Players turn over a $\frac{3}{4}$ card and a $\frac{4}{6}$ card.

The $\frac{3}{4}$ card has a larger shaded area. The player holding the $\frac{3}{4}$ card takes both cards.

$\frac{3}{4}$ $\frac{4}{6}$

EXAMPLE Players turn over a $\frac{1}{2}$ card and a $\frac{4}{8}$ card.

The shaded parts are equal. Each player turns over another card. The player with the larger fraction card takes all the cards.

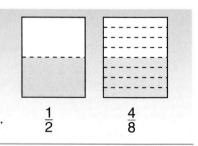

$\frac{1}{2}$ $\frac{4}{8}$

Fraction Top-It (Advanced Version)

Materials ☐ deck of 32 Fraction Cards
(*Math Journal 2,* Activity Sheets 7 and 8)

Players   2

Directions

Put the 32 cards in a stack, picture side down.
Each player takes a card from the top of the deck
but does not turn it over. The shaded sides of
the cards remain facedown.

Take turns. When it is your turn, say whether your
fraction is greater than, less than, or equivalent to
your partner's fraction.

Turn the cards over and compare the shaded parts.
If you were correct, take both cards. If you were
wrong, your partner takes both cards.

The game is over when all cards have been taken
from the stack. The player with more cards wins.

EXAMPLE Joel draws a $\frac{4}{6}$ card. Sue draws a $\frac{1}{3}$
card. It is Joel's turn, and he says that his fraction
is greater than Sue's. They compare shaded areas.
Joel was correct, and he takes both cards.

EXAMPLE Joel draws a $\frac{2}{8}$ card. Sue draws a $\frac{1}{4}$
card. It is Sue's turn, and she says that her fraction
is less than Joel's. They turn the cards over and find
that the shaded areas are equal. The fractions are
equivalent. Sue was wrong, so *Joel* takes both cards.

Less Than You!

Materials ☐ number cards 0–10
(4 of each)

Players 2

Directions

- Deal 2 cards to each player.
- Put the rest of the cards facedown in a pile.
- Take turns.
- On your turn, do the following:

   1. Take the top card from the pile. Now you have 3 cards in your hand.

   2. Discard the highest number in your hand. (Discard means "take out of your hand and put aside.")

   3. Add the two numbers left in your hand.

   4. If you think that your sum is less than the other player's, say "Less than you!"
   If your sum *is* less, you win. If your sum is *not* less, you lose. The game is over.

   5. If you don't say "Less than you!," your turn is over. The game is not over until one of the players says "Less than you!"

Advanced Version Deal 3 cards to each player instead of 2.

Memory Addition/Subtraction

Materials ☐ calculator
Players 2

Directions

1. Players agree on a target number less than 50.

2. Either player clears the calculator's memory. (See **Using the Memory Keys** on the following page.)

3. Players take turns adding 1, 2, 3, 4, or 5 to the calculator's memory or subtracting 1, 2, 3, 4, or 5 from the memory using the (M+) or the (M−) keys. They keep track of the results in their heads. A player cannot use the number that was just used by the other player.

4. The goal is to make the number in memory match the target number. When a player thinks the number in memory is the same as the target number, the player says "Same." Then he or she presses (MRC) to display the number in memory. A player can press (MRC) before or after adding or subtracting a number.

5. If the number in the display matches the target number, the player who said "Same" wins. If the number does not match the target number, that player loses.

Using the Memory Keys

- Press ⊕ to add the number in the display to memory.

- Press ⊖ to subtract the number in the display from memory.

- Press (MRC) once to display the number in memory.

- Press (MRC) twice to clear the memory.

- Change the directions if your calculator works differently.

EXAMPLE   Target number: 19

Winnie presses	Display shows	Maria presses	Display shows
5 (M+)	M 5	4 (M+)	M 4
3 (M+)	M 3	1 (M+)	M 1
2 (M–)	M 2	3 (M+)	M 3
5 (M+) (MRC)	M 19		

Winnie wins.

Missing Terms

Materials   ☐ a calculator for each player
Players   2

Directions

1. Partners enter the same number into both of their calculators.

2. One partner secretly changes this number by adding or subtracting some number.

3. The other partner is shown the new number that appears in the calculator display. He or she guesses what was done to the original number to get the new number.

EXAMPLE   Both calculators are set to 7.

Joyce secretly changes the display by pressing
(+) 9 (=). The display now shows the number 16.

Joyce shows the display number 16 to Al. Al says "You added 9." He is correct.

Multiplication Bingo (Easy Facts)

Materials   ☐ number cards 1–6 and 10 (4 of each)
             ☐ *Multiplication Bingo* Game Mat
                for each player (*Math Masters*,
                p. 120).
             ☐ 8 pennies or other counters
                for each player

Players   2 or 3

Directions

1. The game mat is shown below. You can make your
   own game mat on a piece of paper. Write each of
   the numbers in the list in one of the squares on
   the grid. Don't write the numbers in order.
   Mix them up.

List of Numbers

1	18
4	20
6	24
8	25
9	30
12	36
15	50
16	100

Multiplication Bingo
Game Mat

2. Shuffle the number cards. Place the cards facedown on the table.

3. Take turns. When it is your turn, take the top 2 cards and call out the product of the two numbers. If someone does not agree with your answer, check it by using the Multiplication/ Division Facts Table on page 46 in your *Student Reference Book* or the inside front cover of your journal.

4. If your answer is incorrect, you lose your turn.

5. If your answer is correct and the product is a number on the game mat, place a penny or a counter on that number.

6. If you are the first player to get 4 counters in a row, column, or diagonal, call out "Bingo!" and win the game! You can also call "Bingo!" and win if you get 8 counters anywhere on the game mat.

If all the cards are used before someone wins, shuffle the cards again and keep playing.

EXAMPLES A player could call out "Bingo!" with any of these game mats:

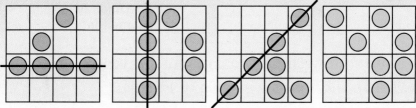

4 counters in a row, column, or diagonal   8 counters anywhere

Multiplication Bingo (All Facts)

Materials   □ number cards 2–9 (4 of each)
□ *Multiplication Bingo* Game Mat
for each player (*Math Masters*, p. 120)
□ 8 pennies or other counters
for each player

Players   2 or 3

Directions

- The game mat is shown below. You can make your
own game mat on a piece of paper. Write each of
the numbers in the list in one of the squares on
the grid. Don't write the numbers in order.
Mix them up.

List of Numbers

24	48
27	49
28	54
32	56
35	63
36	64
42	72
45	81

Multiplication Bingo
Game Mat

- Then follow the directions for playing
Multiplication Bingo (Easy Facts).

2453

Multiplication Draw

Materials ☐ number cards 1–5 and 10 (4 of each)
☐ *Multiplication Draw* Record Sheet
(*Math Masters*, p. 197)

Players 2 or 3

Directions

1. Shuffle the cards. Place them number-side down.

2. Take turns. When it is your turn, draw two cards from the deck to get two multiplication factors. Record both factors and their product on your part of the Record Sheet.

3. After 5 turns, all players find the sums of their five products.

4. The player with the highest sum wins the round.

Harder game: Include cards with numbers 6–9 in the number deck.

EXAMPLE Alex draws a 3 card and a 10 card. He records $3 \times 10 = 30$ on his part of the Record Sheet.

Multiplication Draw Record Sheet

Alex	Round 1	Round 2	Round 3
1st draw:	$3 \times 10 = 30$	$\_\_ \times \_\_ = \_\_$	$\_\_ \times \_\_ = \_\_$
2nd draw:	$\_\_ \times \_\_ = \_\_$	$\_\_ \times \_\_ = \_\_$	$\_\_ \times \_\_ = \_\_$
3rd draw:	$\_\_ \times \_\_ = \_\_$	$\_\_ \times \_\_ = \_\_$	$\_\_ \times \_\_ = \_\_$
4th draw:	$\_\_ \times \_\_ = \_\_$	$\_\_ \times \_\_ = \_\_$	$\_\_ \times \_\_ = \_\_$
5th draw:	$\_\_ \times \_\_ = \_\_$	$\_\_ \times \_\_ = \_\_$	$\_\_ \times \_\_ = \_\_$
Sum of products:	_____	_____	_____

Multiplication Top-It

Materials ☐ number cards 0–10 (4 of each)

Players 2 to 4

Directions

1. Shuffle the cards. Place the deck number-side down on the playing surface.

2. Each player turns over two cards and calls out the product of the numbers.

3. The player with the highest product wins the round and takes all the cards.

4. Play ends when not enough cards are left for each player to have another turn.

5. The player with the most cards wins.

In case of a tie for the highest product, each tied player turns over two more cards and calls out their product. The player with the highest product then takes all the cards from both plays.

EXAMPLE Ann turns over a 6 and a 2. She calls out 12.

Beth turns over a 6 and a 0. She calls out 0.

Joe turns over a 10 and a 4. He calls out 40.

Joe has the highest product. He takes all 6 cards.

EXAMPLE Ann turns over a 3 and an 8.

3 8

She multiplies and calls out 24.

Beth turns over a 4 and a 6.

4 6

She multiplies and calls out 24.

Joe turns over a 9 and a 2.

9 2

He multiplies and calls out 18.

There is a tie. So Ann and Beth each turn over two more cards.

Ann turns over a 3 and a 7.

3 7

She multiplies and calls out 21.

Beth turns over an 8 and a 4.

8 4

She multiplies and calls out 32. Beth takes all 10 cards.

Name That Number

Materials ☐ number cards 0–20 (4 of each card
0–10 and 1 of each card 11–20)

Players 2 to 4 (the game is more interesting
when played by 3 or 4 players)

Directions

1. Shuffle the deck and place five cards faceup on
the playing surface. Leave the rest of the deck
facedown. Then turn over the top card of the deck
and lay the card down. The number on this card
is the number to be named. Call this number the
"target number."

2. Players take turns. When it is your turn, try to
name the target number. You can name the
target number by adding or subtracting the
numbers on 2 of the 5 cards that are faceup.

3. If you can name the target number, take the
2 cards you used to name it. Also take the
target-number card. Then replace all 3 cards
by drawing from the top of the deck.

4. If you cannot name the target number, your turn
is over. Turn over the top card of the deck and lay
it down. The number on this card becomes the
new target number to be named.

5. Play continues until all of the cards in the deck
have been turned over. The player who has taken
the most cards wins.

EXAMPLE Mae and Mike take turns.

| 4 | 10 | 8 | 12 | 2 | | 6 |

It is Mae's turn. The target number is 6. Mae names the number with 4 + 2. She also could have said 8 − 2 or 10 − 4.

Mae takes the 4, 2, and 6 cards. Then she replaces them.

| 7 | 10 | 8 | 12 | 1 | | 16 |

It is Mike's turn. The new target number is 16. Mike cannot find a way to name 16 using 2 cards.

He turns over the next card in the deck and places it on top of 16. This card becomes the new target number. Mike's turn is over.

Advanced Version Players try to name the target number by adding, subtracting, multiplying, or dividing the numbers on as many of their cards as possible.

Number Top-It (5-Digit Numbers)

Materials
- [ ] number cards 0–9 (4 of each)
- [ ] Place-Value Mat (*Math Masters*, pp. 59 and 60)

Players   2 or more

Directions

1. Shuffle the cards. Place the deck number-side down on the playing surface.

2. Each player uses one row of boxes on the Place-Value Mat. Do not use the Millions box or the Hundred-Thousands box.

3. During each round, players take turns turning over the top card from the deck and placing it on any one of the empty boxes. Each player takes 5 turns and places 5 cards on his or her row of the Place-Value Mat.

4. At the end of each round, players read their numbers aloud and compare them. The player with the largest number for the round scores 1 point; the player with the next-larger number scores 2 points; and so on.

5. Players play five rounds per game. When all of the cards in the deck are used, a player shuffles the discarded cards to make a new deck to finish the game. The player with the smallest total number of points at the end of five rounds wins the game.

EXAMPLE The Place-Value Mat below shows the results for one complete round of play, with 4 players.

Place-Value Mat

	Millions	Hundred-Thousands	Ten-Thousands	Thousands	Hundreds	Tens	Ones
John			4	8	6	2	1
Doug			9	3	5	2	0
Sara			4	7	2	0	4
Anju			7	6	6	3	4

Here are the numbers listed from largest to smallest:

Doug	93,520	largest
Anju	76,634	
John	48,621	
Sara	47,204	smallest

Doug scores 1 point for this round. Anju scores 2 points. John scores 3 points. And Sara scores 4 points.

Number Top-It (7-Digit Numbers)

Materials ☐ number cards 0–9 (4 of each)
☐ Place-Value Mat (*Math Masters,* pp. 59 and 60)

Players 2 or more

Directions
This game is played in the same way as *Number Top-It* (5-Digit Numbers). The only difference is that each player uses all 7 boxes in one row of the Place-Value Mat.

In each round, players take turns turning over the top card from the deck and placing it on any one of the empty boxes. Each player takes 7 turns and places 7 cards on his or her row of the game mat.

EXAMPLE Andy and Barb played 7-digit *Number Top-It.* Here is the result for one complete round of play:

Place-Value Mat

	Millions	Hundred-Thousands	Ten-Thousands	Thousands	Hundreds	Tens	Ones
Andy	7	6	4	5	2	0	1
Barb	4	9	7	3	5	2	4

Andy's number is larger than Barb's number. Andy scores 1 point for the round. Barb scores 2 points.

Number Top-It (3-Place Decimals)

Materials ☐ number cards 0–9 (4 of each)
☐ Place-Value Mat for Decimals

Players 2 or more

Directions

This game is played in the same way as *Number Top-It* (5-Digit Numbers). The only difference is that players use the Place-Value Mat for Decimals.

In each round, players take turns turning over the top card from the deck and placing it on any one of the empty boxes. Each player takes 3 turns and places 3 cards on his or her row of the game mat.

EXAMPLE Andy and Barb played *Number Top-It* using the Place-Value Mat for Decimals. Here is the result:

Place-Value Mat for Decimals

	Ones	.	Tenths	Hundredths	Thousandths
Andy	0		3	5	0
Barb	0		6	4	2

Barb's number is larger than Andy's number. Barb scores 1 point for the round. Andy scores 2 points.

Pick-a-Coin

Materials □ regular die
□ calculator for each player
□ *Pick-a-Coin* Record Table
(*Math Masters,* p. 198) for each player

Players   2 or 3

Directions

1. Players take turns. When it is your turn, roll the die five times.

2. After each roll, record the number that comes up on the die in any one of the empty cells on your part of the Record Table.

3. Then use a calculator to find the total amount for that turn.

4. Record the total on the table.

5. After four turns, use your calculator to add the four totals. The player with the largest sum wins.

EXAMPLE   On his first turn, Brian rolled 4, 2, 4, 6, and 1. He filled in his Record Table like this.

Pick-a-Coin Record Table

Player 1	Ⓟ	Ⓝ	Ⓓ	Ⓠ	$1	Total
1st turn	2	1	4	4	6	$7.47
2nd turn						$_.__
3rd turn						$_.__
4th turn						$_.__
					Total	$_.__

Spinning to Win

Materials
☐ paper clip—preferably large (2 in.)
☐ 40 pennies or other counters
☐ spinner (*Math Masters*, p. 182)

Players 2 to 4

Directions

1. The object is to collect the most counters in 12 spins.

2. For each game played, draw a tally chart like the one at the right.

Win 1	Win 2	Win 5	Win 10

3. Each player claims one section of the spinner— 1, 2, 5, or 10. Sections must be different.

4. Players take turns spinning the spinner for a total of 12 spins.

5. For each spin: If the spinner lands on a player's number, the player takes that number of counters. Make a tally mark in the table in the corresponding column to keep track of the spins.

6. The winner is the player with the most counters after 12 spins.

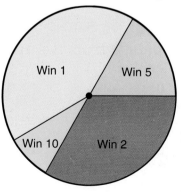

Subtraction Top-It

Materials ☐ number cards 0–20
Players 2–4

Directions

1. Shuffle the cards. Place the deck number-side down on the playing surface.

2. Each player turns over two cards and subtracts the smaller number from the larger number.

3. The player with the largest difference wins the round and takes all the cards.

4. In case of a tie for the largest difference, each tied player turns over two more cards and calls out their difference. The player with the largest difference then takes all the cards from both plays.

5. Play ends when not enough cards are left for each player to have another turn.

6. The player with the most cards wins.

EXAMPLE Ann turns over a 2 and a 14. She subtracts 2 from 14 and calls out 12.

Joe turns over a 10 and a 4. He subtracts 4 from 10 and calls out 6.

Ann has the larger difference. She takes all 4 cards.

EXAMPLE   Ann turns over a 12 and a 6.

| 12 | | 6 |

She subtracts and calls out 6.

Joe turns over a 9 and a 3.

| 9 | | 3 |

He subtracts and calls out 6.

There is a tie. So both players turn over two more cards.

Ann turns over a 10 and an 8.

| 10 | | 8 |

She subtracts and calls out 2.

Joe turns over a 7 and a 3.

| 7 | | 3 |

He subtracts and calls out 4. Joe takes all 8 cards.

Three Addends

Materials ☐ number cards 0–20 (4 of each card
0–10 and 1 of each card 11–20)

☐ *Three Addends* Record Sheet for each
player (*Math Masters*, p. 33, optional)

Players 2

Directions

1. Shuffle the cards and place the deck number-side
down on the playing surface.

2. One player draws three cards from the top of the
deck and turns them over.

3. You and your partner write addition models using
the three numbers.

4. You can write your addition number model on the
record sheet or on a separate sheet of paper.

5. List the numbers in any order you wish. Try to
list the numbers so that it is easy to add them.

6. Then add the numbers and compare your answer
to your partner's answer.

Some other ways to play the game

- Give the sum of the numbers showing without
writing down number models.

- Draw four cards from the deck. Turn them
over and find the sum of the four numbers.

Data Bank

Drinks Vending Machine Poster

EXAMPLE The "Exact Change" light is on and you want to buy grape juice.

• Use any combination of coins that equals 45 cents.

The "Exact Change" light is not on and you want to buy grape juice.

• If you use a dollar bill, the machine will give you the grape juice and 55 cents in change.

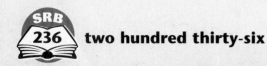

Vending Machine Poster

Stationery Store Poster

$1.79

SALE! Reg. $1.89

Correction Fluid

$2.99

SALE! Reg. $4.49

Pens Box of 24

$3 off

Photo Album

Paper Clips Box of 100

99¢ SALE! Reg. $1.39

$1.49 SALE! Reg. $1.89

Pencils Box of 24

$2.99 SALE! Reg. $5.19

Batteries 8-Pack

99¢ SALE! Reg. $1.89

Crayons

BUY-RITE COUPON

49¢ **Notebook**

Without coupon 99¢

Variety Store Poster

Toys

Fashion

- **Mini stock cars**
  10 per box   **$2.99** per box

- **Marbles**
  45 per bag   **$1.45** per bag

- **Interlocking building blocks**
  395 pieces   **$19.99** per set

- **Bright shoelaces**
  5 pairs per package   **$2.99** per pkg.

- **Ponytail rings**
  12 per package   **$1.77** per pkg.

- **"Hair Things"**
  6 per bag   **$1.00** per pkg.

School Supplies

Notebook paper   **$0.98** per pkg.
200 sheets per package

Value Pack pens
10 in a package   **$1.27** per pkg.

Chocolate scented pens!
6 in a pack   **$1.29** per pack

File cards
100 in a pack   **$1.69** per pack

"Fashion" pens   *4 for* **$1.29**

Brilliant color markers
5 in a package   **$1.99**

Scented markers
8 in a pack   **$2.69**

Pencils   *8-pack* **$1.00**
   6-pack **$0.69**

Party Supplies

Glitter Stickers
7 per pack   **$1.00** per pack

9-inch balloons
25 per bag   **$1.99** per bag

Party hats   *6 for* **$1.49**

Party horns   *8 for* **$2.99**

Giant 14-inch balloons
package of 5 for **$1.79**

Stock-Up Sale Poster #1

1 Light Bulbs **$1.09**
4-Pack

5 OR MORE SALE	You pay $0.88 per 4-pack

2 VCR Tape **$3.25**

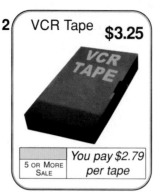

5 OR MORE SALE	You pay $2.79 per tape

3 Tissues **$0.73**

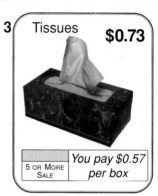

5 OR MORE SALE	You pay $0.57 per box

4 Transparent Tape **$0.84**

5 OR MORE SALE	You pay $0.65 per roll

5 Batteries **$3.59**
4-Pack

5 OR MORE SALE	You pay $2.90 per pack

6 Toothpaste **$1.39**

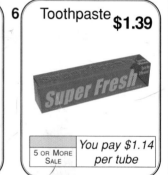

5 OR MORE SALE	You pay $1.14 per tube

7 Ballpoint Pen **$0.39**

5 OR MORE SALE	You pay $0.27 per pen

8 Tennis Balls **$2.59**
Can of 3

5 OR MORE SALE	You pay $1.86 per can

9 Paperback Book **$2.99**

Max
Goes to Florida

5 OR MORE SALE	You pay $2.25 per book

Stock-Up Sale Poster #2

1 Greeting Cards

Box of 12 **$3.29**

5 OR MORE SALE	You pay $2.63 per box

2 Bath Soap **$0.88**

5 OR MORE SALE	You pay $0.65 per bar

3 Gift Wrapping Paper **$2.35**

per roll

5 OR MORE SALE	You pay $1.86 per roll

4 Toothbrush **$1.38**

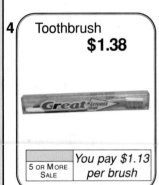

5 OR MORE SALE	You pay $1.13 per brush

5 Video Stories **$3.75**

5 OR MORE SALE	You pay $3.18 per tape

6 Night Light Bulbs

2-Pack **$0.96**

5 OR MORE SALE	You pay $0.76 per box

7 Audio Tape

60 Minutes **$2.47**

5 OR MORE SALE	You pay $1.97 per tape

8 Construction Paper **$0.67**

per pad

5 OR MORE SALE	You pay $0.54 per pad

9 Pair of shoelaces **$1.27**

per pair

5 OR MORE SALE	You pay $1.08 per pair

Animal Clutches

All of the animals shown lay eggs. A nest of eggs is called a *clutch*.

Most birds, reptiles, and amphibians lay eggs once or twice a year. Insects may lay eggs daily during a certain season of the year.

Green Turtle
(up to 1.5 meters long)
median of 104 eggs,
as many as 184 eggs

Ostrich
(more than
2 meters tall)
up to 15 eggs

Giant Toad
(up to 30 cm long)
normal maximum of
35,000 eggs

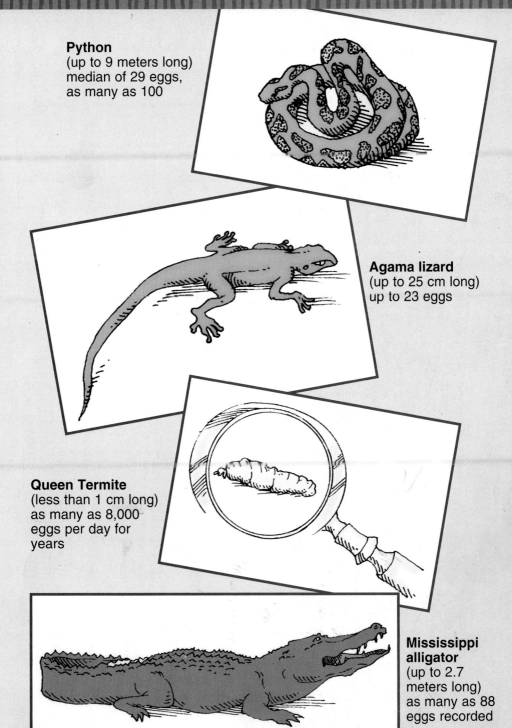

Python
(up to 9 meters long)
median of 29 eggs,
as many as 100

Agama lizard
(up to 25 cm long)
up to 23 eggs

Queen Termite
(less than 1 cm long)
as many as 8,000
eggs per day for
years

**Mississippi
alligator**
(up to 2.7
meters long)
as many as 88
eggs recorded

Normal Spring High and Low Temperatures (in °F)

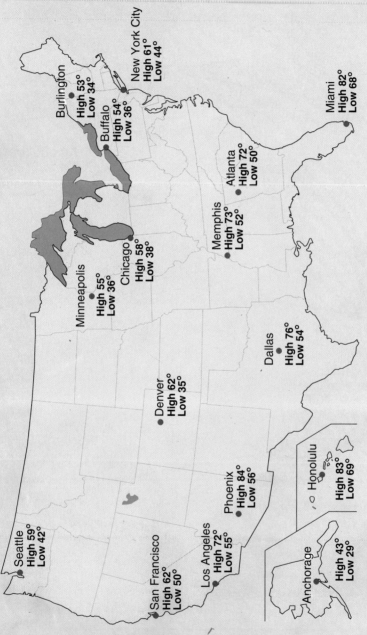

New York City
High 61°
Low 44°

Burlington
High 53°
Low 34°

Buffalo
High 54°
Low 36°

Miami
High 82°
Low 68°

Atlanta
High 72°
Low 50°

Memphis
High 73°
Low 52°

Chicago
High 58°
Low 38°

Minneapolis
High 55°
Low 36°

Dallas
High 76°
Low 54°

Denver
High 62°
Low 35°

70° is normal room temperature

Honolulu
High 83°
Low 69°

Phoenix
High 84°
Low 56°

Seattle
High 59°
Low 42°

San Francisco
High 62°
Low 50°

Los Angeles
High 72°
Low 55°

Anchorage
High 43°
Low 29°

September Rainfall

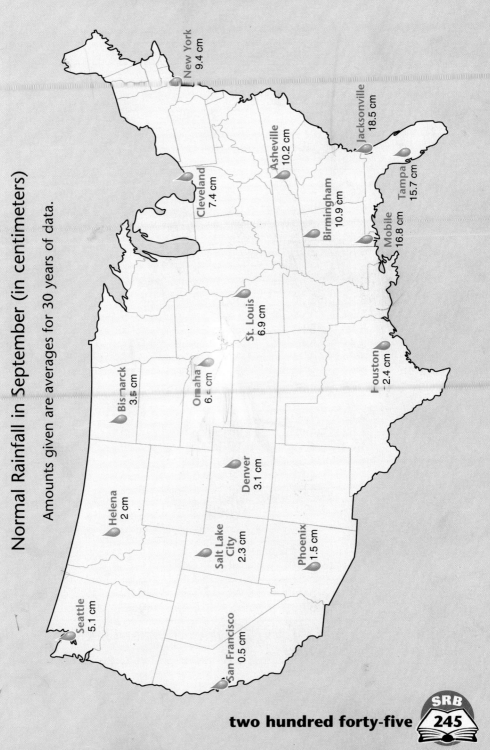

Normal Rainfall in September (in centimeters)

Amounts given are averages for 30 years of data.

New York
9.4 cm

Jacksonville
18.5 cm

Asheville
10.2 cm

Cleveland
7.4 cm

Tampa
15.7 cm

Birmingham
10.9 cm

Mobile
16.8 cm

St. Louis
6.9 cm

Bismarck
3.5 cm

Omaha
6.= cm

Houston
=.4 cm

Denver
3.1 cm

Helena
2 cm

Salt Lake
City
2.3 cm

Phoenix
1.5 cm

Seattle
5.1 cm

San Francisco
0.5 cm

Shipping Packages: Rate Table

Ground Service						
Residential Deliveries						
(Delivery to a home)						

WEIGHT NOT TO EXCEED	ZONES						
	2	**3**	**4**	**5**	**6**	**7**	**8**
1 lb	$2.53	$2.67	$2.87	$2.95	$3.03	$3.10	$3.16
2	2.55	2.69	3.12	3.21	3.40	3.50	3.72
3	2.64	2.85	3.29	3.43	3.67	3.84	4.13
4	2.73	2.98	3.41	3.59	3.86	4.07	4.45
5	2.83	3.09	3.48	3.66	4.01	4.24	4.66
6	2.93	3.17	3.53	3.71	4.11	4.41	4.81
7	3.03	3.23	3.58	3.76	4.21	4.58	5.05
8	3.13	3.28	3.63	3.82	4.34	4.83	5.42
9	3.22	3.36	3.68	3.91	4.53	5.15	5.83
10	3.31	3.44	3.73	4.08	4.76	5.48	6.20
11	3.39	3.53	3.81	4.31	5.02	5.83	6.65
12	3.47	3.63	3.92	4.52	5.34	6.18	7.08
13	3.54	3.74	4.09	4.74	5.63	6.56	7.52
14	3.61	3.86	4.27	4.96	5.92	6.91	7.96
15	3.68	4.00	4.45	5.19	6.20	7.28	8.40
16	3.75	4.15	4.63	5.43	6.51	7.64	8.83
17	3.82	4.29	4.81	5.64	6.79	8.00	9.27
18	3.89	4.42	4.98	5.87	7.08	8.37	9.70
19	4.00	4.55	5.16	6.08	7.39	8.73	10.14
20	4.13	4.69	5.34	6.32	7.67	9.08	10.58
21	4.27	4.83	5.52	6.55	7.96	9.46	11.02
22	4.38	4.98	5.69	6.76	8.25	9.81	11.46
23	4.50	5.10	5.87	6.99	8.55	10.17	11.88
24	4.61	5.25	6.04	7.21	8.84	10.54	12.33
25	4.72	5.37	6.21	7.44	9.12	10.91	12.76
26	4.82	5.52	6.40	7.67	9.43	11.25	13.20
27	4.93	5.67	6.58	7.89	9.71	11.63	13.65
28	5.00	5.81	6.75	8.11	10.01	11.99	14.07
29	5.09	5.94	6.93	8.34	10.30	12.35	14.53
30	5.20	6.06	7.12	8.59	10.63	12.75	15.01

FOR ANY FRACTION OF A POUND OVER THE WEIGHT SHOWN, USE THE NEXT HIGHER RATE.

Shipping Packages: Zone Map

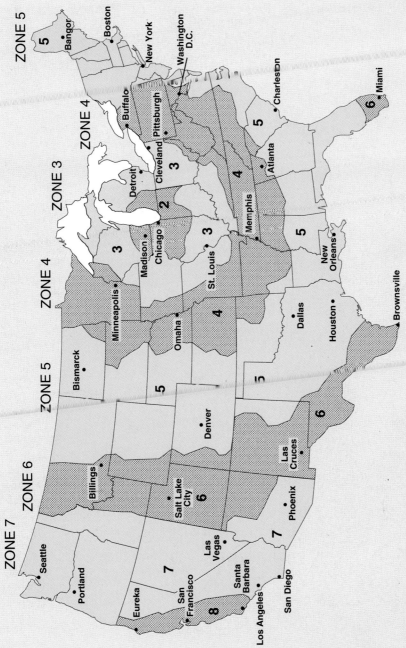

U.S. Road Mileage Map

Except for Hawaii and Alaska, all numbers are highway distances in miles.

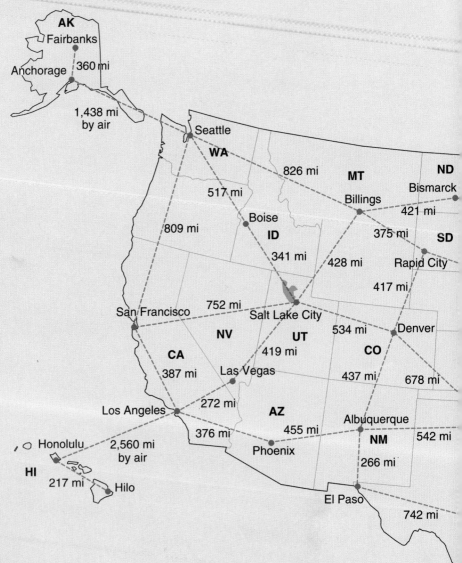

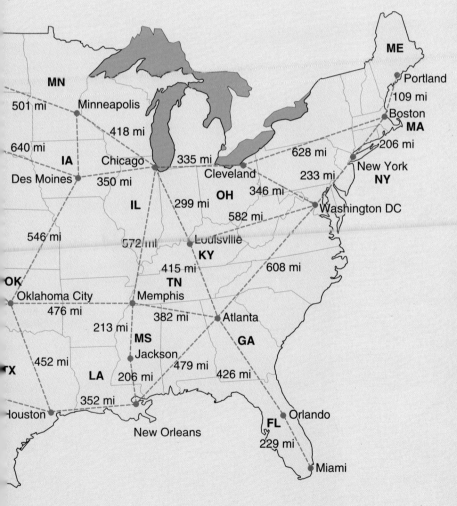

Major U.S. City Populations

Tacoma
179,114

Las Vegas
376,906

Denver
497,840

Los Angeles
3,553,638

Phoenix
1,159,014

San Diego
1,171,121

Dallas
1,053,292

Houston
1,744,05

1995 U.S. Census data

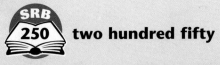

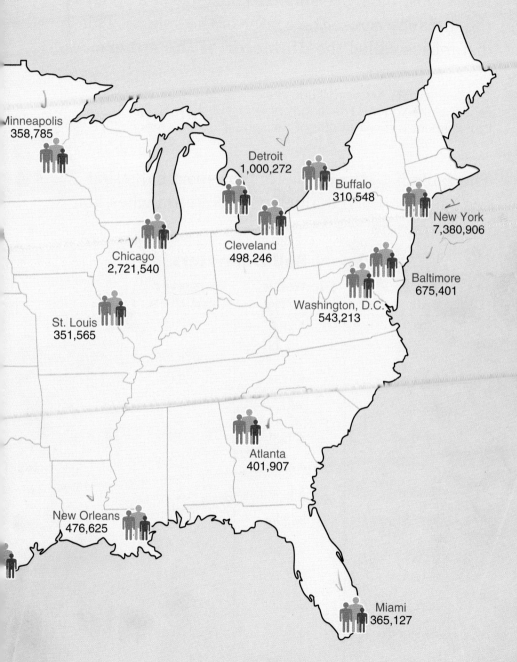

Minneapolis
358,785

Detroit
1,000,272

Buffalo
310,548

New York
7,380,906

Chicago
2,721,540

Cleveland
498,246

Baltimore
675,401

Washington, D.C.
543,213

St. Louis
351,565

Atlanta
401,907

New Orleans
476,625

Miami
365,127

Sizes of Sport Balls

Most sport balls are spheres. The size of a sphere is the distance across the center of the sphere. This distance is called the **diameter of the sphere.**

The segment *RS* passes through the center of the sphere. The length of this segment is the diameter of the sphere.

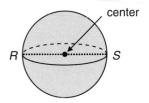

The table lists the diameters for sport balls that are spheres. Each diameter is given in inches and in centimeters.

Sport Ball Diameters

Ball	Diameter in Inches	Diameter in Centimeters
Table tennis	$1\frac{1}{2}$ in.	3.8 cm
Squash	$1\frac{5}{8}$ in.	4.1 cm
Golf	$1\frac{11}{16}$ in.	4.3 cm
Tennis	$2\frac{5}{8}$ in.	6.7 cm
Baseball	$2\frac{3}{4}$ in.	7.0 cm
Cricket	$2\frac{13}{16}$ in.	7.1 cm
Croquet	$3\frac{5}{8}$ in.	9.2 cm
Softball	$3\frac{13}{16}$ in.	9.7 cm
Volleyball	$8\frac{1}{4}$ in.	21.0 cm
Bowling	$8\frac{1}{2}$ in.	21.8 cm
Soccer	$8\frac{3}{4}$ in.	22.2 cm
Water polo	$8\frac{7}{8}$ in.	22.5 cm
Basketball	$9\frac{1}{2}$ in.	24.1 cm

Weights of Sport Balls

The table below lists the weights for sport balls. Each weight is given in ounces and in grams.

Reminder: 16 ounces equals 1 pound
1,000 grams equals 1 kilogram

Sport Ball Weights

Ball	Weight in Ounces	Weight in Grams
Table tennis	$\frac{1}{10}$ oz	2.5 g
Squash	$\frac{9}{10}$ oz	25 g
Golf	$1\frac{1}{2}$ oz	43 g
Tennis	2 oz	57 g
Baseball	5 oz	142 g
Cricket	$5\frac{1}{2}$ oz	156 g
Softball	$6\frac{1}{2}$ oz	184 g
Volleyball	$9\frac{1}{2}$ oz	270 g
Soccer	15 oz	425 g
Water polo	15 oz	425 g
Croquet	16 oz	454 g
Basketball	22 oz	625 g
Bowling	56 oz	1,590 g

Source: *Rules of the Game,* Diagram Group, 1990 (rev 1995 paper).

Some interesting questions

1. Which balls weigh 1 pound or more?

2. Which balls weigh 1 kilogram or more?

3. Are the heaviest balls also the balls with the largest diameters?

two hundred fifty-three SRB 253

Physical Fitness Standards

The table on the opposite page shows data for three fitness tests.

Curl-Ups

A partner holds your feet. You cross your arms and place your hands on opposite shoulders. You raise your body and curl up to touch your elbows to your thighs. Then you lower your back to the floor. This counts as one curl-up. Do as many curl-ups as you can in one minute.

One Mile Run/Walk

You cover a 1-mile distance in as short a time as you can. You may not be able to run the entire distance. Walk when you are not able to run.

Arm Hang

Hold the bar with your palms facing away from your body. Your chin should clear the bar. (See the picture.) Hold this position as long as you can.

Physical Fitness Test Scores
(median scores for each age)

	Age	Curl-Ups (in 1 minute)	1-Mile Run (minutes:seconds)	Arm Hang (seconds)
	6	22	12:36	6
B	7	28	11:40	8
O	8	31	11:05	10
Y	9	32	10:30	10
S	10	35	9:48	12
	11	37	9:20	11
	12	40	8:40	12
	6	23	13:12	5
G	7	25	12:56	6
I	8	29	12:30	8
R	9	30	11:52	8
L	10	30	11:22	8
S	11	32	11:17	7
	12	35	11:05	7

Source: "The National Physical Fitness Award: Qualifying Standards."

EXAMPLE The table shows 31 curl-ups for 8-year-old boys. 31 curl-ups is the median score for 8-year-old boys. About half of all 8-year-old boys will do more than 31 curl-ups, and about half of all 8-year-old boys will do fewer than 31 curl-ups.

EXAMPLE The table shows a time of 12 minutes and 30 seconds for 8-year-old girls in the mile run. About half of all 8-year-old girls will take longer than 12:30 to run a mile, and about half of all 8-year-old girls will take less than 12:30.

Record High and Low Temperatures

The table shows the highest and lowest temperatures ever recorded in each state.

State Record Temperatures (in degrees Fahrenheit)

State	Lowest °F	Highest °F	State	Lowest °F	Highest °F
Alabama	−27	112	Missouri	−40	118
Alaska	−80	100	Montana	−70	117
Arizona	−40	128	Nebraska	−47	118
Arkansas	−29	120	Nevada	−50	125
California	−45	134	N. Hampshire	−46	106
Colorado	−61	118	New Jersey	−34	110
Connecticut	−32	105	New Mexico	−50	122
Delaware	−17	110	New York	−52	108
District			N. Carolina	−34	110
of Columbia	−15	106	N. Dakota	−60	121
Florida	−2	109	Ohio	−39	113
Georgia	−17	112	Oklahoma	−27	120
Hawaii	12	100	Oregon	−54	119
Idaho	−60	118	Pennsylvania	−42	111
Illinois	−35	117	Rhode Island	−23	104
Indiana	−36	116	S. Carolina	−19	111
Iowa	−47	118	S. Dakota	−58	120
Kansas	−40	121	Tennessee	−32	113
Kentucky	−34	114	Texas	−23	120
Louisana	−16	114	Utah	−69	117
Maine	−48	105	Vermont	−50	105
Maryland	−40	109	Virginia	−30	110
Massachusetts	−35	107	Washington	−48	118
Michigan	−51	112	W. Virginia	−37	112
Minnesota	−59	114	Wisconsin	−54	114
Mississippi	−19	115	Wyoming	−66	114

Source: *The World Almanac and Book of Facts 1999*, pp. 223 and 224.

Tornado Data

Tornadoes are violent storms.
A tornado looks like a narrow
black cloud that is shaped like
a funnel. The funnel reaches
down toward the ground. The
tip of the funnel touches the
ground as it moves along.

The winds of a tornado can
reach speeds of 500 miles per hour.

Nearly all tornadoes occur in the United States.
Tornadoes are very common in some states. But
some states hardly ever have tornadoes.

Tornado Map for 1995–2000

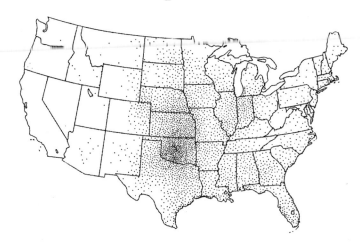

Each tornado that occurred between 1995 and
2000 is shown by a dot. The dot marks the spot
where the tornado first touched the ground.

Source: From *The Handy Science Answer Book*, by The Carnegie Library of Pittsburgh, published by Visible Ink Press, copyright 1994. Reprinted by permission of The Gale Group.

World Population Growth

There are more than 6 billion people in the world today. The table and graph below show how the world's population has grown.

By the year 2050, the world will have about 10 billion people.

World Population Table

Date	Population	Date	Population
8000 B.C.	6,000,000	1900	1,633,000,000
A.D. 1	250,000,000	1950	2,515,000,000
1000	250,000,000	1960	3,019,000,000
1250	416,000,000	1970	3,698,000,000
1500	460,000,000	1980	4,450,000,000
1600	579,000,000	1990	5,292,000,000
1700	679,000,000	2000	6,261,000,000
1800	954,000,000		

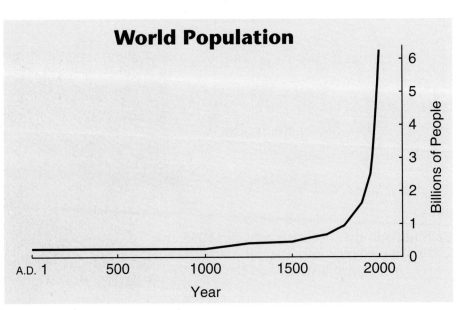

World Population

Heights of 8-Year-Old Children

The table below shows heights that were measured to the nearest centimeter. All of the boys and girls were 8 years old.

Third Graders' Heights

Boys		Girls	
Boy	Height	Girl	Height
#1	136 cm	#1	123 cm
#2	129 cm	#2	141 cm
#3	110 cm	#3	115 cm
#4	122 cm	#4	126 cm
#5	126 cm	#5	122 cm
#6	148 cm	#6	144 cm
#7	127 cm	#7	127 cm
#8	126 cm	#8	133 cm
#9	124 cm	#9	120 cm
#10	142 cm	#10	125 cm
#11	118 cm	#11	126 cm
#12	130 cm	#12	107 cm

The average 8-year-old boy is slightly taller than the average 8-year-old girl. How can you use the data in the table to show this?

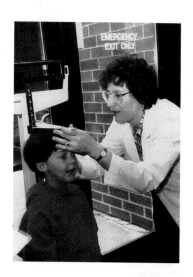

Head Size

Your head size is the distance around your head. You can use a tape measure to measure the distance around. The line graph on the opposite page shows how head size increases as you get older. The graph shows the *median* head size for each age.

EXAMPLE The graph shows a *median* head size of 52 centimeters for an 8-year-old. About half of all 8-year-olds have a head size *larger* than 52 cm. And about half have a head size *smaller* than 52 cm.

Describe what happens to a baby's head size during the first year of its life. Is your head growing as fast as a baby's head?

Ask someone to measure your head size. Use the centimeter scale of the tape measure. Compare your head size to the median head size for your age. Is your head larger than the median head size or smaller than the median head size?

Median Head Size

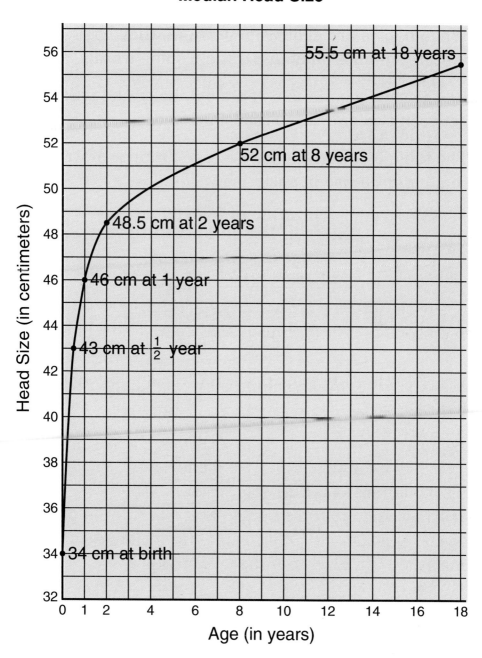

Head Size (in centimeters)

Age (in years)

55.5 cm at 18 years

52 cm at 8 years

48.5 cm at 2 years

46 cm at 1 year

43 cm at $\frac{1}{2}$ year

34 cm at birth

Number of Words Children Know

When babies are about one year old, they begin to imitate sounds. They understand some words.

By the time a child is 6 years old, he or she uses between two and three thousand words.

The table below gives the average number of words that children use in speaking.

Number of Words Children Use in Speaking

Age in Years	Number of Words
1	3
$1\frac{1}{2}$	22
2	272
$2\frac{1}{2}$	446
3	896
$3\frac{1}{2}$	1,222
4	1,540
$4\frac{1}{2}$	1,870
5	2,072
6	2,562

Source: *Discovering Psychology,* B. Weiner, Chicago: Science Research Assn., p. 97.

Letter Frequencies

There are 26 letters in the English alphabet. Some letters (like E and T) are used quite often. Other letters (like Q and Z) are not used very much.

The table below shows how often each letter is used in writing English words. If you looked at 1,000 letters, you could expect to see about this number of each letter.

Letter Frequencies

82	As	70	Ns
14	Bs	80	Os
28	Cs	20	Ps
38	Ds	1	Q
130	Es	68	Rs
30	Fs	60	Ss
20	Gs	105	Ts
53	Hs	25	Us
65	Is	9	Vs
1	J	15	Ws
4	Ks	2	Xs
34	Ls	20	Ys
25	Ms	1	Z

Some interesting questions

Which 5 letters are used the most? The least?

The letters A, E, I, O, and U are called *vowels*. How many vowels would you expect to see if you looked at 1,000 letters?

Heights and Depths

The tables below show the highest point on each continent and the deepest ocean depths.

Continent	Highest point	Feet
Asia	Mount Everest, Nepal-Tibet	29,028
South America	Mount Aconcagua, Argentina	22,834
North America	Mount McKinley, U.S.A.	20,320
Africa	Kilimanjaro, Tanzania	19,340
Europe	Mount El'brus, Russia	18,510
Antarctica	Vinson Massif, Sentinal Rouge	16,864
Australia	Mount Kosciusko, New South Wales	7,310

Ocean depths	Feet
Pacific Ocean	−36,200
Atlantic Ocean	−30,246
Indian Ocean	−24,442
Arctic Ocean	−17,881

Other places in the U.S. are above or below sea level. Negative heights (−) are below sea level.

Mount Hood

Location	Feet
Mt. Whitney, California	14,494
Death Valley, California	−282
Mauna Kea, Hawaii	13,796
Mount Hood, Oregon	11,239
Highest point in Louisiana	535
New Orleans, Louisiana	−8
Mount Katahdin, Maine	5,267
Highest point in S. Dakota	7,242

How Much Would You Weigh on the Moon?

All objects are attracted to each other by a force known as "gravity." Gravity pulls your body toward the center of the Earth.

When you weigh yourself, you step on a scale. The reading on the scale measures the pull of Earth's gravity on your body.

The pull of the moon's gravity is much less than the pull of Earth's gravity. You would weigh much less on the moon. The table shows how a person's weight would change if people could travel to the planets, sun, and moon. The weights are for a space traveler who weighs 100 pounds on Earth.

Weight Changes for a Space Traveler

Location	Person's Weight
Earth	100 pounds
Moon	17 pounds
Sun	2,790 pounds
Mercury	37 pounds
Venus	88 pounds
Mars	38 pounds
Jupiter	264 pounds
Saturn	115 pounds
Uranus	115 pounds
Neptune	112 pounds
Pluto	4 pounds

Source: *The World Almanac and Book of Facts 1997*, R. Famighetti, ed., New Jersey: World Almanac Books, p. 455.

Ages of U.S. Presidents

The table below gives the age of each man when he became president.

President	Age	President	Age
1. George Washington	57	22. Grover Cleveland	47
2. John Adams	61	23. Benjamin Harrison	55
3. Thomas Jefferson	57	24. Grover Cleveland	55
4. James Madison	57	25. William McKinley	54
5. James Monroe	58	26. Theodore Roosevelt	42
6. John Quincy Adams	57	27. William Taft	51
7. Andrew Jackson	61	28. Woodrow Wilson	56
8. Martin Van Buren	54	29. Warren Harding	55
9. William Harrison	68	30. Calvin Coolidge	51
10. John Tyler	51	31. Herbert Hoover	54
11. James Polk	49	32. Franklin Roosevelt	51
12. Zachary Taylor	64	33. Harry Truman	60
13. Millard Fillmore	50	34. Dwight Eisenhower	62
14. Franklin Pierce	48	35. John Kennedy	43
15. James Buchanan	65	36. Lyndon Johnson	55
16. Abraham Lincoln	52	37. Richard Nixon	56
17. Andrew Johnson	56	38. Gerald Ford	61
18. Ulysses Grant	46	39. James Carter	52
19. Rutherford Hayes	54	40. Ronald Reagan	69
20. James Garfield	49	41. George Bush	64
21. Chester Arthur	51*	42. William Clinton	46

*Some resources list Chester Arthur as having been born October 5, 1829; others say 1830. He became president (after the death of Garfield) September 20, 1881. At that time he was either 50 or 51 years old.

Who was the youngest person to become president? Who was the oldest person?

Railroad Timetable and Airline Schedule

Train Schedule for a Chicago Rail Line

Airline Schedule, Chicago to New York

Station	Time	Departure	Arrival
South Chicago	11:46 A.M.	6:00 A.M.	8:59 A.M.
83rd Street	11:49	6:20 A.M.	1:12 P.M.*
Cheltenham	11:51	7:00 A.M.	9:56 A.M.
South Shore	11:55	7:00 A.M.	10:04 A.M.
Bryn Mawr	11:57	8:00 A.M.	11:00 A.M.
59th Street	12:04 P.M.	8:45 A.M.	2:00 P.M.*
Hyde Park	12:08	9:00 A.M.	12:00 P.M.
Kenwood	12:09	10:00 A.M.	12:58 P.M.
McCormick Place	12:14	10:20 A.M.	3:19 P.M.*
18th Street	12:15	11:00 A.M.	1:55 P.M.
Van Buren Street	12:19	12:00 P.M.	3:00 P.M.
Randolph Street	12:22	1:00 P.M.	3:55 P.M.
		1:20 P.M.	4:21 P.M.
		1:20 P.M.	6:45 P.M.*
		1:30 P.M.	4:39 P.M.
		2:00 P.M.	5:09 P.M.
		3:00 P.M.	6:04 P.M.
		4:00 P.M.	7:00 P.M.
		4:14 P.M.	9:19 P.M.*
		4:40 P.M.	7:30 P.M.
		5:00 P.M.	8:01 P.M.
		6:00 P.M.	9:02 P.M.
		7:00 P.M.	10:00 P.M.

* Flight makes other stops.

The times shown are local times.
New York time is 1 hour ahead of Chicago time.

More Information about North American Animals

North America

- 3rd largest continent (only Asia and Africa are larger)

- $\frac{1}{6}$ of the world's land area

- 9,406,000 square miles

- $\frac{1}{20}$ of the world's total area (total area equals land area plus water area)

- $2\frac{1}{2}$ times larger than the United States

Although the animals on journal pages 206 and 207 are positioned on or near areas they inhabit, their natural habitats may greatly exceed the locales in which they are shown. Below is more information about the ranges of these animals.

American alligator	Coastal areas of Florida, Alabama, Mississippi, and Texas
American porcupine	North America except Arctic region
Arctic fox	Arctic regions; tundras of North America and Europe
Atlantic green turtle	Temperate and tropical regions of the Atlantic Ocean
Beaver	North America except Arctic regions, Florida, southwestern United States, and northern Mexico
Beluga whale	Arctic coasts of North America, Asia, and Europe
Black bear	Canada; and parts of the United States
Bottle-nosed dolphin	Coastal and open waters of the world's oceans
Common dolphin	Coastal and open waters of the world's oceans
Gila monster	Southwestern United States and northern Mexico
Gray fox	Southern Canada to northern South America
Gray whale	Northern Pacific Ocean
Harp seal	Arctic waters of the Atlantic Ocean as far south as Maine
Mountain goat	Western United States and Canada
Northern fur seal	Northern part of the Pacific Ocean
Pilot whale	Northern regions of the Atlantic Ocean
Polar bear	Arctic coastal waters and ice floes
Puma	Western regions of North America
Raccoon	Southern Canada to Panama
Right whale	Worldwide coastal waters
Sea otter	California coast and Bering Sea
Snowshoe hare	Northern United States and Canada
Walrus	Arctic regions
West Indian manatee	Caribbean waters; Florida coasts
White-tailed deer	Southern Canada to northern South America

Source: *Do Elephants Eat Too Much?* Robert Balfanz. Everyday Learning Corp., 1992.

Tables of Measures

Metric System

Units of Length

1 kilometer (km) = 1,000 meters (m)

1 meter (m) = 10 decimeters (dm)

= 100 centimeters (cm)

= 1,000 millimeters (mm)

1 decimeter (dm) = 10 centimeters (cm)

1 centimeter (cm) = 10 millimeters (mm)

Units of Area

1 square meter – 10,000 square (sq m)   centimeters (sq cm)

1 square centimeter = 100 square (sq cm)   millimeters (sq mm)

Units of Volume

1 cubic meter = 1,000,000 cubic (cu m)   centimeters (cu cm)

1 cubic centimeter = 1,000 cubic (cu cm)   millimeters (cu mm)

Units of Capacity

1 kiloliter (kL) = 1,000 liters (L)

1 liter (L) = 1,000 milliliters (mL)

Units of Mass (Weight)

1 metric ton (t) = 1,000 kilograms (kg)

1 kilogram (kg) = 1,000 grams (g)

1 gram (g) = 1,000 milligrams (mg)

U.S. Customary System

Units of Length

1 mile (mi) = 1,760 yards (yd)

= 5,280 feet (ft)

1 yard (yd) = 3 feet (ft)

= 36 inches (in.)

1 foot (ft) = 12 inches (in.)

Units of Area

1 square yard = 9 square feet (sq yd)   (sq ft)

= 1,296 square inches (sq in.)

1 square foot = 144 square (sq ft)   inches (sq in.)

Units of Volume

1 cubic yard = 27 cubic feet (cu yd)   (cu ft)

1 cubic foot = 1,728 cubic (cu ft)   inches (cu in.)

Units of Capacity

1 gallon (gal) = 4 quarts (qt)

1 quart (qt) = 2 pints (pt)

1 pint (pt) = 2 cups (c)

1 cup (c) = 8 fluid ounces (fl oz)

1 fluid ounce = 2 tablespoons (fl oz)   (tbs)

1 tablespoon = 3 teaspoons (tbs)   (tsp)

Units of Mass (Weight)

1 pound (lb) = 16 ounces (oz)

1 ton (T) = 2,000 pounds (lb)

Units of Time

1 millennium	= 10 centuries
	= 100 decades
	= 1,000 years (yr)
1 century (cent)	= 10 decades
	= 100 years (yr)
1 year (yr)	= 12 months (mo)
	= 52 weeks (wk) plus 1 or 2 days
	= 365 or 366 days

1 month (mo)	= 28, 29, 30, or 31 days
1 week (wk)	= 7 days
1 day	= 24 hours (hr)
1 hour (hr)	= 60 minutes (min)
1 minute (min)	= 60 seconds (sec)

Units of Body Measure

1 **digit** is about the width of a finger.

1 **hand** is about the width of the palm and thumb.

1 **span** is about the distance from the tip of the thumb to the tip of the little finger of outstretched hand.

1 **cubit** is about the length from the elbow to the tip of the outstretched fingers.

1 **yard** is about the distance from the tip of the nose to the end of the thumb of an outstretched arm.

1 **fathom** is about the length from fingertip to fingertip of outstretched arms.

Systems Equivalents

1 inch is about 2.5 centimeters.

1 kilometer is about 0.6 mile.

1 mile is about 1.6 kilometers.

1 meter is about 39 inches.

1 liter is about 1.1 quarts.

1 ounce is about 28 grams.

1 kilogram is about 2.2 pounds.

A.M. An abbreviation that means "before noon." It refers to the period between midnight and noon.

Angle A figure that is formed by two rays or two line segments that have the same endpoint.

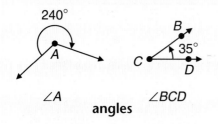

∠A   ∠BCD

angles

Apex In a pyramid or cone, the vertex opposite the base.

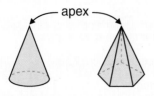

Area The amount of surface inside a shape. Area is measured in square units, such as square inches or square centimeters.

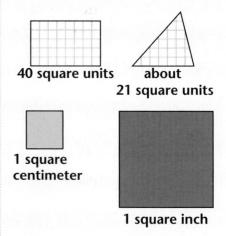

40 square units   about 21 square units

1 square centimeter

1 square inch

Array An arrangement of objects in rows and columns.

array

B **C**

Ballpark estimate
A good, rough estimate.
A ballpark estimate can
be used when you don't
need an exact answer or
to check if an answer
makes sense.

Bar graph A graph that
uses bars to represent
numbers in the data.

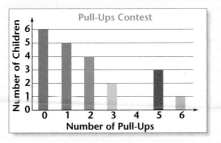

Base A name used for
a side of a polygon and
a face of a 3-dimensional
figure.

Bases are shown in blue.

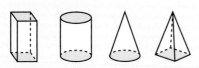

Bases are shown in blue.

Capacity The amount
a container or scale can
hold.

Celsius The temperature
scale used in the metric
system.

Center The point inside
a circle or sphere that is
the same distance from
all of the points on the
the circle or sphere.

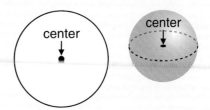

Chance The possibility that something will occur. For example, when you flip a coin, there is an equal chance of getting heads or tails.

Change number story A number story in which an amount is increased (a change-to-more story) or decreased (a change-to-less story). A change diagram can be used to keep track of the numbers and missing information in such problems.

Start	Change	End
14	−5	?

$$14 - 5 = ?$$

Circle A curved line that forms a closed path on a flat surface so that all points on the path are the same distance from a point called the *center*.

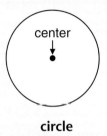

circle

Circumference The distance around a circle, or its perimeter.

Comparison number story A number story in which two quantities are compared. A comparison diagram can be used to keep track of the numbers and missing information in such problems.

Quantity
12

Quantity	Difference
9	?

12 − 9 = ? or 9 + ? = 12

Composite number
A counting number that has more than 2 factors. For example, 4 is a composite number because it has 3 factors: 1, 2, and 4.

Cone A solid that has a circular base and a curved surface that ends at a point called the *apex*.

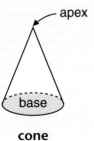

apex

base

cone

Congruent figures
Figures that have the same shape and same size.

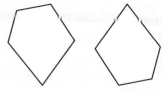

congruent pentagons

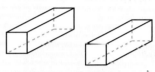

congruent prisms

Coordinate grid A grid formed by drawing two number lines that form right angles. The number lines intersect at their zero points. Coordinate grids can be used to locate points that are identified by numbers in ordered pairs called *coordinates*. Maps are often based on coordinate grids.

ordered pair

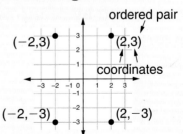

(−2,3)   (2,3)

coordinates

(−2,−3)   (2,−3)

coordinate grid

Counting numbers The numbers used in counting: 1, 2, 3, 4, and so on. Zero is sometimes thought of as a counting number.

Cylinder A solid that has two circular bases that are parallel and the same size. The bases are connected by a curved surface. A can and a paper towel roll are examples of cylinders.

cylinder

D

Data Information that is collected by counting, measuring, asking questions, or observing.

Decimal A number, such as 13.4, that contains a decimal point. Money amounts, such as $7.89, are decimal numbers. The decimal point in money separates the dollars from the cents.

Degree A unit of measure for angles. Also a unit of measure for temperature.

Denominator The number below the line in a fraction. For example, in $\frac{3}{4}$, 4 is the denominator.

Diameter A line segment that goes through the center of a circle and has endpoints on the circle. Also, the length of this line segment. The diameter of a sphere is defined in the same way.

Digits The symbols 0, 1, 2, 3, 4, 5, 6, 7, 8, and 9 that are used to write any number in our number system.

Edge A line segment or curve where the surfaces of a solid meet.

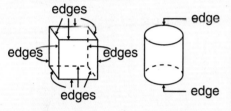

Endpoint The point at the end of a ray or line segment.

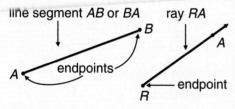

Equal-grouping story A number story in which a total collection is separated into equal groups. A diagram can be used to keep track of the numbers and missing information in such problems.

teams	players per team	players in all
6	9	?

Equal-sharing story A number story in which a group of things is divided into equal parts, called *shares*. A diagram can be used to keep track of the numbers and missing information in such problems.

piles	cards por pile	cards in all
4	?	24

Equilateral triangle A triangle with all three sides the same length and all three angles the same measure.

equilateral triangle

Equivalent names Different ways of naming the same number. For example, 2 + 6, 4 + 4, 12 − 4, 100 − 92, 5 + 1 + 2, eight, VIII, and ~~HH~~ /// are equivalent names for 8.

Estimate 1.) An answer that is close to an exact answer. 2.) To calculate an answer that is close, but not exact.

Even number Any counting number that can be divided by 2 with no remainder. For example, 2, 4, 6, and 8 are all even numbers.

Event Something that happens. Tossing heads with a coin and rolling a 3 with a die are events.

Face A flat surface on the outside of a solid.

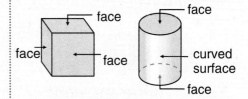

Fact family 1.) Related addition and subtraction facts. For example, 5 + 6 = 11, 6 + 5 = 11, 11 − 5 = 6, and 11 − 6 = 5 are a fact family. 2.) Related multiplication and division facts. For example, 5 × 7 = 35, 7 × 5 = 35, 35 ÷ 5 = 7, and 35 ÷ 7 = 5 are also a fact family.

Fact Triangles Cards with a triangle shape that show fact families. Fact Triangles are used like flash cards to help you memorize basic addition, subtraction, multiplication, and division facts.

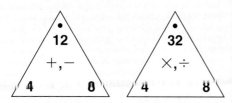

Factors 1.) Any of the numbers that are multiplied to find a product. For example, in the problem $4 \times 7 = 28$, 28 is the product, and 4 and 7 are the factors. 2.) A number that divides another number evenly. For example, 8 is a factor of 24.

Facts table A chart with rows and columns that shows all of the basic addition and subtraction facts or all of the basic multiplication and division facts.

Fahrenheit The temperature scale used in the U.S. customary system.

Fractions. A number in the form $\frac{a}{b}$ or a/b, where a is called the *numerator* and b is called the *denominator*. (The denominator cannot be 0.) One use for fractions is to name part of a whole or part of a collection.

Frames and Arrows A diagram used in *Everyday Mathematics* to show a number pattern or sequence.

Function machine
An imaginary machine used in *Everyday Mathematics* to change numbers according to a given rule.

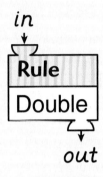

in	out
1	2
3	6
5	10
10	20
100	200

Geometry The study of shapes.

Geometric solids
Three-dimensional shapes, such as prisms, pyramids, cylinders, cones, and spheres.

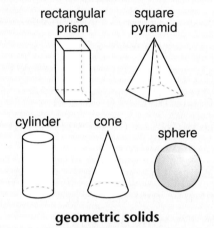

geometric solids

Intersect To meet or cross.

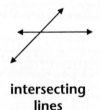

intersecting lines

K

Kite A 4-sided polygon
with two pairs of equal
sides. The equal sides
are next to each other.
The four sides cannot
all have the same length.
(So a rhombus is not
a kite.)

kite

L

Lattice method One
method for solving
multiplication problems.

Line A straight path
that goes on forever in
both directions.

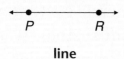

line

Line graph A graph
that uses line segments
to connect data points.
Line graphs are often
used to show how
something has changed
over a period of time.

**Attendance for the
First Week of School**

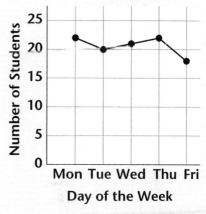

Line plot A sketch of
data that uses Xs,
checks, or other marks
above a number line to
show how many times
each value appeared in
the set of data.

two hundred eighty-one **281**

Line segment
A straight path between two endpoints.

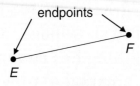

endpoints

F

E

line segment

Line symmetry
A figure has line symmetry if a line can divide it into two parts that look exactly like, but are facing in opposite directions. The dividing line is called the *line of symmetry.*

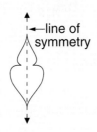

←line of symmetry

Maximum The largest number in a set of data.

Mean An average number in a set of data. The mean is found by adding all of the data values and then dividing by the number of numbers in the set of data.

Median The middle number in a set of data when the numbers are put in order from smallest to largest, or largest to smallest. The median is also known as the *middle number* or *middle value.*

Metric system
A measuring system that is used by scientists everywhere and in most countries in the world except the United States. The metric system is a decimal system. It is based on multiples of 10. See the Table of Measures on pages 270 and 271.

Minimum The smallest number in a set of data.

Mode The number or value that occurs most often in a set of data.

Name-collection box In *Everyday Mathematics,* a place to write equivalent names for the same number.

| 25 | 37 − 12 | 20 + 5 |

~~HHT~~ ~~HHT~~ ~~HHT~~ ~~HHT~~ ~~HHT~~

twenty-five

veinticinco

X X X X X
X X X X X
X X X X X
X X X X X
X X X X X

name-collection box

Negative number A number that is less than zero.

Number grid A table that lists numbers in order.

Number line A line with numbers marked in order on it.

Number model A number sentence that shows how a number story can be solved. For example, 10 − 6 = 4 is a number model for the following story: I had 10 brownies. I gave 6 away. How many did I have left?

Numerator The number above the line in a fraction. For example, in $\frac{3}{4}$, 3 is the numerator.

Odd number Any counting number that cannot be exactly divided by 2. When an odd number is divided by 2, there is always a remainder of 1. For example, 1, 3, 5, and 7 are all odd numbers.

Ordered pair A pair of numbers, such as (5,3) or (1,4), used to find a location on a coordinate grid. The numbers in an ordered pair are called *coordinates*. See *coordinate grid* for a diagram.

Parallel Always the same distance apart, and never meeting or crossing each other, no matter how far extended.

parallel lines

Parallelogram A 4-sided polygon that has 2 pairs of parallel sides. The parallel sides are also the same length.

parallelogram

Partial-products method One method for solving multiplication problems.

Partial-sums method One method for solving addition problems.

Parts-and-total number story A number story in which two parts are combined to find a total. A parts-and-total diagram can be used to keep track of the numbers and missing information in such problems.

Total	
?	
Part	**Part**
8	5

$8 + 5 = ?$

Pattern Shapes or numbers that repeat in a regular way so that what comes next can be predicted.

Per "For each" or "in each." For example, "three tickets per student" means "three tickets for each student."

Perimeter The distance around a shape.

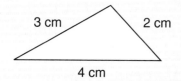

perimeter =
4 cm + 3 cm + 2 cm = 9 cm

Place value The system for writing numbers in which the value of a digit depends on its place in the number.

P.M. An abbreviation that means "after noon." It refers to the period between noon and midnight.

Point An exact location in space.

Polygon A closed figure on a flat surface that is made up of line segments joined end to end. The line segments of a polygon may not cross.

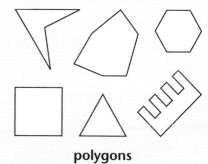

polygons

Polyhedron A geometric solid whose surfaces, or faces, are all formed by polygons.

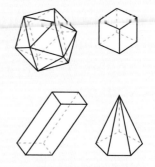

polyhedrons

Positive number A number that is greater than zero.

Prime number
A counting number that has exactly two factors that are counting numbers: itself and 1. For example, 5 is a prime number because its only two factors are 5 and 1.

Prism A solid that has two parallel bases that are polygons with the same size and shape. The other faces are parallelograms. They are often rectangles. Prisms get their names from their bases. For example, if a prism has bases that are triangles it is called a *triangular prism*.

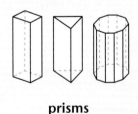

prisms

Probability A number between 0 and 1 that is used to tell the chance of something happening.

Pyramid A solid that has one base that is a polygon. All of the other sides, or faces, are triangles that come together at a point called the *vertex* or *apex*. Pyramids get their names from their bases. For example, if a pyramid has a base that is a hexagon it is called a *hexagonal pyramid*.

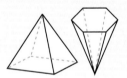

pyramids

Q   R

Quadrangle A polygon that has four sides and four angles. Same as *quadrilateral*.

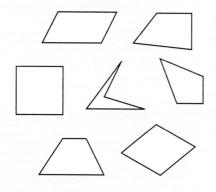

quadrangles or quadrilaterals

Quadrilateral A polygon that has four sides and four angles. Same as *quadrangle*.

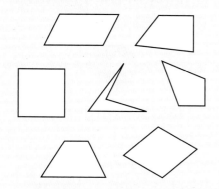

quadrangles or quadrilaterals

Radius A line segment that goes from the center of a circle to any point on the circle. Also, the length of this line segment. The radius of a sphere is defined the same way.

Range The difference between the biggest (maximum) and the smallest (minimum) numbers in a set of data.

Ray A straight path that has one endpoint and goes on forever.

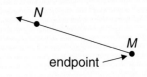

Rectangle

A parallelogram whose corners are all right angles.

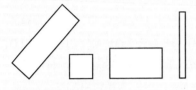

rectangles

Remainder

The amount left over when things are divided or shared equally. Sometimes there is no remainder.

Rhombus

A parallelogram with all four sides the same length.

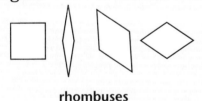

rhombuses

Right angle A 90° angle.

Its sides form a square corner.

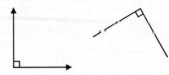

right angles

Right triangle

A triangle with one 90° angle.

right triangle

Round To adjust

a number to make it easier to work with. Often, numbers are rounded to the nearest 10, 100, 1,000, etc.

Scale drawing

A drawing that represents an actual object or region but is

a different size. Maps are scale drawings.

Side Any of the line segments that make up a polygon. Sometimes, a face of a solid figure is also called a side.

Sphere A solid with a curved surface that looks like a ball or a globe. The points on a sphere are all the same distance from a point called the *center*.

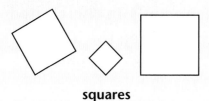

sphere

Square A rectangle whose sides are all the same length.

squares

Standard units Measurement units that are the same size no matter who uses them and when or where they are used.

Tally chart A chart that uses tally marks to show how many times each value appears in a set of data.

Number of Pull-Ups	Number of Children
0	⌁⌁⌁ /
1	⌁⌁⌁
2	////
3	//
4	
5	///
6	/

tally chart

Temperature A measure of how hot or cold something is.

Three-dimensional
Solid objects that take up space, such as boxes, balls, and containers, are 3-dimensional.

Trade-first method
One method for solving subtraction problems.

Trapezoid A 4-sided polygon with exactly one pair of parallel sides.

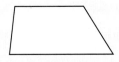

trapezoid

Triangle A polygon that has three sides and three angles.

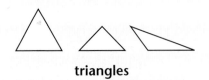

triangles

Turn-around facts
Numbers can be added or multiplied in either order. $3 + 5 = 8$ and $5 + 3 = 8$ are turn-around addition facts. $4 \times 5 = 20$ and $5 \times 4 = 20$ are turn-around multiplication facts. There are no turn-around facts for subtraction and division if the numbers are different.

Two-dimensional
Flat shapes that take up area, but not space, are 2-dimensional. For example, rectangles, triangles, circles, and other shapes drawn on paper or a flat surface are 2-dimensional.

●●●●●● **U** ●●●●●●●

U.S. customary system
A measurement system that is used most commonly in the United States. See the Table of Measures on pages 270–271.

Vertex The point where the rays of an angle or the sides of a polygon or the edges of a polyhedron meet.

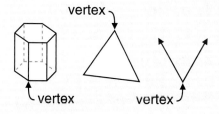

vertex

vertex

vertex

Volume The amount of space inside a three-dimensional object. Volume is usually measured in cubic units, such as cubic centimeters or cubic inches. Sometimes it is measured in units of capacity, such as gallons or liters.

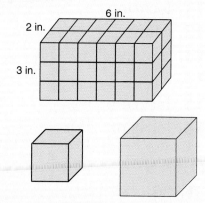

6 in.

2 in.

3 in.

1 cubic centimeter   1 cubic inch

Weight A measure of how heavy something is.

Answer Key

Page 5
1. measure
2. code
3. count
4. location
5. comparison
6. measure
7. location
8. measure
9. count
10. comparison
11. location
12. count
13. location
14. count
15. location
16. location

Page 9
1. 35
2. a.

		88	89
96	97	98	

b.

314		316	317
	325	326	

Page 12
1.

| 50 | $50\frac{1}{3}$ | $50\frac{2}{3}$ | 51 | $51\frac{1}{3}$ | $51\frac{2}{3}$ | 52 |

Page 15
6

Page 17
1. a. 26　　b. 200
   c. 11　　d. 12
2. a. $(20 - 8) + 3 = 15$
   b. $20 = 5 + (3 \times 5)$
   c. $3 \times (6 + 13) = 57$
   d. $2 \times (3 + 1) \times 2 = 16$

Page 21
1. 274, 284, 294, 304, 314, 324, 334, 344, 354, 364
2. 61,087
3. a. 6,473　b. 10,870
4. a. 3,561　b. 982
5. 643

Page 23

1. a. $\frac{2}{3}$ **b.** $\frac{3}{16}$ **c.** $\frac{0}{3}$

2. a. $\frac{1}{2}$; one-half

   b. $\frac{4}{9}$; four-ninths

   c. $\frac{6}{10}$; six-tenths

   d. $\frac{8}{8}$; eight-eighths

Page 29

1. Sample answers:

$\frac{2}{4}$; $\frac{3}{6}$; $\frac{4}{8}$

2. Sample answers:

$\frac{2}{3}$; $\frac{4}{6}$; $\frac{8}{12}$

Page 32

1. >

2. <

3. =

4. <

5. =

6. <

7. close to 0

8. close to 1

9. close to 0

10. close to 0

11. close to 0

12. close to 1

Page 34

1. $\frac{30}{100}$; 0.30

2. $\frac{85}{100}$; 0.85

Page 36

1. 2.7   **2.** 0.5

3. 0.84   **4.** 1.7

Page 49

1. a. $4 + 9 = 13$
$9 + 4 = 13$
$13 - 4 = 9$
$13 - 9 = 4$

b. $6 \times 8 = 48$
$8 \times 6 = 48$
$48 \div 6 = 8$
$48 \div 8 = 6$

2. a.

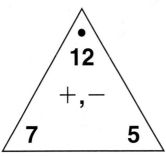

b.

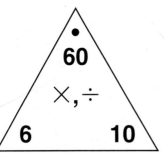

Page 59

1. 322

2. 552

3. 12,565

4. 3,354

Page 62

1.

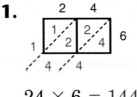

$24 \times 6 = \underline{144}$

2.

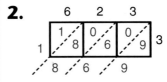

$623 \times 3 = \underline{1,869}$

3.

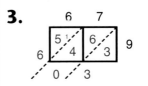

$67 \times 9 = \underline{603}$

4.

$56 \times 47 = \underline{2,632}$

Page 70

1. 3

2. Tomato juice; water

Page 72
1. a. Friday
   b. Tuesday
   c. 3 children
   d. 25 children

2.

Number Correct

Page 76
1. Minimum: 23
   Maximum: 43
   Range: 20
2. a. 5
   b. Minimum: 0
   Maximum: 10
   Range: 10
3. 6

Page 79
1. 16
2. 8

Page 83
1. a. 60 degrees
   b. 40 degrees
   c. Saturday and
   Sunday
   d. 50 degrees because
   that is the median
   temperature
   e. 7

2.

Number of Hits

Page 95
1. triangle, pentagon
2. a. hexagon
   b. quadrangle
   c. octagon
   d. dodecagon

Page 101
1. 1 in.
2. $1\frac{1}{4}$ in.
3. $\frac{1}{2}$ in.

Page 110
triangle C

Page 112
1.

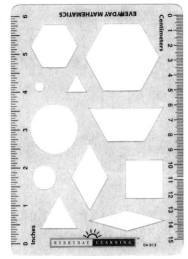

2. Sample answers:
Infinite; many

Page 118
1. a. 100 **b.** 10 **c.** 1,000

2. millimeter; gram;
meter; centimeter

3. a. 4 cm line

_____

b. 40 mm line

_____

c. Both line segments
are the same length.

Page 124
1. 10,000 meters
2. a. 300 cm **b.** 350 cm
3. 7 cm
4. meters
5. a. 2 km   **b.** 2,000 m
6. 2.5 cm

Page 127
1.

_____

2. $3\frac{2}{4}$ or $3\frac{1}{2}$ in.
3. a. $\frac{1}{2}$ in.   **b.** 1 in.
   c. $1\frac{3}{4}$ in. **d.** $2\frac{3}{8}$ in.
   e. $3\frac{1}{8}$ in. **f.** $3\frac{1}{2}$ in.

Page 131
1. a. 21   **b.** 24
   c. 2   **d.** 72
2. 57 inches
3. 12
4. 100 yd; 300 ft
5. 6 miles

Page 133
1. 15 ft
2. 60 mm
3. 39 in.

Page 135
1. 21 mm
2. 63 mm
3. 36 in.

Page 138
1. 14 square cm
2. 27 square in.
3. 1 square meter

Page 141
1. 1 cubic meter
2a. 9 cu cm
 b. 10 cu in.
 c. 60 cu ft

Page 143
1. a. 12 **b.** 3   **c.** 3
2. 40 cups
3. 40 fluid ounces

Page 145
1. yes

Page 146
1. 1 gram
 1 ounce
 1 pound
 1 kilogram
2. a. 1   **b.** 1
 c. 1,000 **d.** 0.6
 e. 160   **f.** 4

Page 155
1. a. 100 **b.** 32 **c.** 98.6
 d. 20   **e.** −18
2. 26 °F
3. 80 °C
4. 38 °F

Page 157
1. before noon and after noon
2. 12:00 A.M.; 2:55 A.M.; 4:15 A.M.; 10:50 A.M.; 12:00 P.M.; 3:05 P.M.; 7:30 P.M.; 9:45 P.M.
3. 10 years
4. 300 years
5. 24
6. 28
7. 3,600 seconds

Page 159
1. April; June; September; November
2. Monday
3. May 22
4. Friday, August 4

Page 161

1. Sample answer:
Mar. 21 to June 20

2. Houston has about 4 more hours of sunlight than Seward on December 22.

Page 163

1. a. B **b.** J

2. a. (2, 2) **b.** (5, 7)

3. b. (6, 4) **c.** (5, 0)
  d. (3, 1) **e.** $(4, 5\frac{1}{2})$
  f. $(1\frac{1}{2}, 2\frac{1}{2})$

Page 170

1. 60

2. 10

3. 50

4. 600

5. 6,000

6. 300 + 50 = 350

Page 173

1.

2.

Page 184

1. Each friend got 6 pennies.

2. The perimeter of the rectangle is 80 cm.

3. Each pencil cost 12¢.

4. The numbers are 3 and 4.

5. There are 14 boys in the class.

A

Abbreviations
  for metric system units, 116,
    119, 142, 144
  for divisions of a day, 156, 272,
    285
  for U.S. customary system
    units, 125, 128, 142
Addition
  column method, 53
  fact triangles, 48
  facts table, 44
  games for, 194, 202, 215, 234
  partial-sums method, 51–52
A.M., 156, 272
Angle measurer, 149–150
Angles
  congruent, 109
  definition of, 90, 92, 272
  game for, 195
  history of measurement, 149
  measuring, 90, 149
  notation, 90
  of triangles, 96
  sides of, 90
  vertex of, 90
Animal clutches, 242–243
Answer keys, 292–298
Apex, 107, 272, 286
Area
  definitions of, 136–137, 272
  of rectangles, 136, 138
  of squares, 136
  surface, 136–137, 272
  units for measuring, 270
Arrays
  definition of, 63, 272
  for equal groupings, 64, 66
  games for, 197, 207
  in division, 207
  in multiplication, 58
Arrows, 176
Average, 77–79, 282

B

Ballpark estimate, 167–168, 273
Bar graphs, 80, 273
Base-10 blocks
  for addition, 52
  for volume measures, 139
  for weight measures, 144–145
Bases, 273
  of geometric solids, 105–107, 286
Billions, 41, 42
Billionths, 42
Body parts, units for measuring, 271
Boxes
  in Frames-and-Arrows
    diagrams, 176
  on calendars, 6
  name-collection, 14

C

Calculators
  addition on, 202, 215, 217, 230
  displays on, 206
  games for, 202–203, 206, 215,
    217, 230
  memory on, 216
  multiplication on, 203
  subtraction on, 215, 217
Calendars, 6, 158–159
Capacity
  definition of, 273
  metric units for, 142, 270
  of scales for weight measures,
    146
  U.S. customary units for, 142,
    270
  volume of containers, 142
Celsius scale, 11, 273
Center
  of a circle, 100, 273, 274, 276
  of a sphere, 108, 273, 289
Centimeters, 117, 119, 122–123
Century, 156
Chance, 26, 84–86, 274
Change-number stories, 186, 274
Circles, 100–101
  as bases of cylinders, 107
  center of, 100, 273–274, 276
  circumference of, 134, 274
  congruent, 110
  definition of, 100, 274
  diameter of, 100, 134, 276
  for comparing fractions, 27

Circumference of a circle, 134, 274
Column method of addition, 53
Columns
    in arrays, 63, 272
    in tables and charts, 44
    of numbers in addition, 53
Comparison diagram, 190, 275
Comparison number stories, 190,
    274
Comparisons
    of decimals, 36
    of fractions, 27
    of capacity, 142
    of different systems' units, 145
    of weight, 144
    of whole numbers, 4, 274
    with place-value charts, 20, 36
Composite numbers, 37–38, 275
Cones, 107, 275
Congruent figures, 109–110, 275
Coordinate grids, 162, 275
Coordinates, 162, 275
Counting numbers
    definition of, 2, 276
    even/odd, 38
    factors of, 37, 38
    names of very large and very
        small, 41–42
    place value in, 18–19
Counting-up method of subtraction,
    57
Counts, 2
Cubes, 41, 42, 65, 102, 104
Cubic centimeters, 42, 139
Cubic millimeters, 41, 42
Cubic units for measuring, 41, 42,
    139
Cubit, 114
Cups, 142
Cylinders, 103, 107, 276

D

Data
    definition of, 70, 276
    describing a set of, 73–75
    methods for collecting, 70
    organizing, 70–71
    recording, 70–71, 80, 82

Data Bank, 235–271
    clutches of eggs, 242–243
    head sizes, 260–261
    heights and depths of
        continents and oceans, 264
    heights of 8-year-olds, 259
    letter frequencies in English
        language, 263
    measurement tables 270–271
    mileage map of the U.S.,
        248–249
    North American animals,
        268–269
    number of words children
        know, 262
    physical fitness standards,
        254–255
    populations of U.S. cities,
        250–251
    rainfall in the U.S., 245
    sports ball sizes and weights,
        252–253
    stationery store poster, 238
    stock-up sale posters, 240–241
    tables of measures, 270–271
    temperatures in the U.S., 244,
        256
    timetables for railroad and
        airline, 267
    tornadoes, 257
    U.S. presidents' ages, 266
    variety store poster, 239
    vending machine posters,
        236–237
    weights and zones for shipping
        packages, 246–247
    weights on the moon, 265
    world population growth, 258
Day, 156, 160
Decade, 156
Decimal point, 33, 35, 276
Decimals
    as money, 33, 35
    comparing, 36
    definition of, 276
    for measuring, 3
    game for, 229
    names for, 33–34
    notation for, 33, 35

place value in, 35–36
place value chart for, 35–36
renaming fractions as, 33–34
to show probability, 85
Degrees
Celsius, 116, 152
definition of, 276
Fahrenheit, 152
history of measuring circles
with, 149
in angle measurements, 90
in temperature measurements,
4, 11, 39, 152
notation for 3–5, 11, 90, 149,
152
on a circle, 149
Denominators, 11, 22, 31–32,
276
Diameter,
of a circle, 100, 276
of a sphere, 108, 276
Difference, 8, 154, 190
Digits, 18, 35, 277
Distance key on a map, 164
Division
equal grouping in, 68
equal sharing in, 67
fact triangle, 49
facts table, 46–47
for equal-groups problems,
192
game for, 207
notation for, 67
of fractions, 29
stories for equal sharing, 67
Dodecahedron, 104
Dot picture patterns, 24, 58, 64,
174–175
Drinks Vending Machine poster,
236

E

Earth
diameter of, 108
distance from the sun, 42
distance from the surface to the
center of, 108
locations on the surface of, 3

revolution around the sun, 158
size of, 108
Edges of a solid, 103, 107, 277
Endpoints,
of line segments, 88, 92,
276–277, 282
of rays, 89, 92, 277
on a number line, 11
on triangles, 96
Equal, 13, 15
Equal groups
definition of, 64, 277
diagrams for problems, 191
in division, 68, 207
in multiplication, 65
with arrays, 64, 66, 207
Equal-grouping story, 277
Equal-sharing division stories, 67,
277
Equilateral triangle, 97, 277
Equivalent fractions, 27–30,
212–213
Equivalent names, 14, 278
Estimates, 166–170
ballpark, 167
definition of, 166, 278
to solve number stories, 182
Estimation, 166–170
Even numbers, 9, 38, 174, 278
Event, 84, 278

F

Faces
definition of, 278
of prisms, 106
of pyramids, 105
of solids, 102
Fact families, 48–49, 278
Facts tables
addition/subtraction, 44–45
definition of, 279
multiplication/division, 46–47
Fact triangles, 48–49, 279
Factors, 37–38, 210, 279
Fahrenheit scale, 279
Fathom, 114
Fluid ounces, 142
Foot measure, 114, 116, 128, 130

Fraction cards, 31–32, 212–213
Fractions
    as division lines on rulers, 125–126
    as negative numbers, 4
    definition of, 279
    division of, 29
    equivalent, 27–30, 208–209
    for comparing numbers, 26, 31
    for describing chance, 26
    for naming part of a collection, 24
    for naming parts of a whole, 22
    in measurements, 3, 25
    in number comparisons, 26, 31
    multiplication of, 29
    notation for, 22
    on a number line, 11, 26
    parts of, 22
    renaming as decimals, 33–34
    to show probability, 85
    uses of, 22–32
Frames, 176
Frames-and-Arrows diagram, 176–177, 279
Function machines, 178–180, 280

G

Gallons, 142
Games, 194–234
    Addition Top-It, 194
    Angle Race, 195
    Array Bingo, 197
    Baseball Multiplication, 198–201
    Beat the Calculator, 202–203
    The Block-Drawing Game, 204–205
    Broken Calculator, 206
    Division Arrays, 207
    Equivalent Fractions, 208–209
    Factor Bingo, 210–211
    Fraction Top-It, 212–213
    Less Than You!, 214
    Memory Addition/Subtraction, 215–216
    Missing Terms, 217
    Multiplication Bingo, 218–220
    Multiplication Draw, 221
    Multiplication Top-It, 222–223
    Name That Number, 224–225
    Number Top-It, 226–229
    Pick-a-Coin, 230
    Spinning to Win, 231
    Subtraction Top-It, 232
    Three Addends, 234
Geometric solids
    cone, 103
    cubes, 102–103
    cylinders, 102–103, 107
    definition of, 102, 280
    parts of, 102–103, 105–108
    polyhedrons, 104–106
    prisms, 104, 106
    pyramids, 104–105
    spheres, 108
Geometry
    angles, 90
    circles, 100
    congruent figures, 109
    cylinder, 107
    definition of, 88, 280
    endpoints, 88, 89
    line segments, 88, 92, 93
    line symmetry, 111
    lines, 89, 92, 93
    parallel lines/segments, 91
    polygons, 94–99
    quadrangles, 98-99
    rays, 89, 92, 93
    shapes in, 88
    solids, 102–108
    triangles, 96–97
Googol, 41
Gram, 116
Graphs
    bar, 80, 81, 273
    line, 82, 281
Greater-than comparisons, 13, 31, 213

H

Hand measurement, 114
Head sizes, 260–261
Heights/depths of continents and oceans, 264
Heights of 8-year-olds, 259
Heptagon, 95

Hexagon, 95
Hexagonal Prism, 106
History of
    angle measurement, 149
    measuring degrees in a circle,
      149
    measurement units, 114
    the metric system, 116
    numbers, 18
    place value, 18
Hours, 156
Hundredths, 33

I

Icosahedron, 104
Inch scale, 119
Inches, 116, 119, 125, 128, 130
Intersect, 91, 94, 280
Intersecting lines/segments, 91,
    93–94, 280

K

Kilograms, 144
Kilometers, 122–123
Kite, 99, 281

L

Lattice method of multiplication,
    60–62, 281
Leap year, 156, 158
Left-to-right method of subtraction,
    56
Length
    changing units of, 122, 128–129
    comparing units of, 122, 128
    in metric units, 116, 119, 270
    in U.S. customary units,
      116–117, 125, 128
    of days, 160–161
    personal reference tables for,
      123, 130
    table of units for measuring,
      270
Less-than comparisons, 13, 31,
    213–214
Letter frequencies in English, 263

Light, speed of, 42
Line graphs, 82, 281
Line plots, 71, 75, 281
Line segments, 88, 91–93, 109,
    276, 282
Line symmetry, 111, 282
Lines
    definition of, 89, 92, 281
    intersecting, 91
    naming of, 89
    notation for, 88–91
    parallel, 91
Liters, 142
Locations, 3

M

Mass, 270
Math operations with parentheses,
    16–17
Maximum, 73, 282, 287
Mean, 77–79, 282
Median, 282
Measurement
    Celsius scale of, 11, 116
    degrees in, 276
    history of, 114
    metric system for, 116–123, 282
    metric units for, 11, 142, 144
    of angles, 90, 149–150
    of circles, 100–101
    of the Earth, 108
    of temperatures, 4, 11, 116, 289
    of weight, 144
    of volume, 291
    perimeter, 132–133
    systems equivalents table, 271
    tables of units for, 142,
      270–271
    tools, 11, 25
    U.S. customary system for,
      116–117, 144, 290
    using body parts for, 271
    using decimals in, 3
    using fractions in, 3, 25
    using numbers for, 2
    using rulers for, 11, 25

Measures, 2
Meter, 116, 122–123
Meterstick, 117, 119
Metric system
    abbreviations for units in, 116,
        119, 122
    area in, 270
    capacity in, 270
    Celsius scale, 11, 116
    conversions in, 122
    decimal base for, 117, 282
    definition of, 282
    history of, 116
    length in, 116, 119, 122, 270
    personal references for length
        in, 123
    temperature in, 116
    volume, 270
    weight (mass), 116, 144, 270
    units in, 270
    uses for, 116, 119
Metric ton, 144
Middle number, 74
Middle value, 74
Midnight, 156
Miles, 128, 130
Millennium, 156
Milligrams, 144
Milliliters, 142
Millimeters, 117, 119, 122–123
Millions, 41
Minimum, 73, 283, 287
Minute, 156
Mode, 75, 283
Money
    decimals in, 33, 276
    estimating amounts needed,
        166–167
    game for, 230
    notation for, 33
    place value for dollars and
        cents, 35
Months, 156
Multiplication
    arrays in, 66
    equal groupings in, 65
    fact triangle, 49
    factors in, 37

facts table, 46–47
for equal-groups problems, 191
games for, 198, 200, 203,
    218–223
lattice method, 60 62
    history of, 62
notation for, 65
number models of problems in,
    66
of fractions, 29
on calculators, 203
partial-products method of,
    58–59
product of, 37
to make rectangular numbers,
    175
to make square numbers, 175
with fact triangles, 49

N

Name-collection boxes, 14–15, 283
    equivalent names in, 14
Nanosecond, 42
Negative numbers
    definition of, 39, 283
    for temperatures, 4, 11, 39, 152
    in a number grid, 40
    on number lines, 10, 39–40
Nonagon, 95
Noon, 156
North American animals, 268–269
Notation for
    addition, 48
    angles, 90
    decimals, 33, 35, 67
    degrees, 3–5, 11, 90, 149, 152
    division, 67
    equal to, 13, 15
    fractions, 22
    greater than, 13, 31
    less than, 13, 31
    line segments, 88
    lines, 89
    money, 33
    multiplication, 49, 65
    negative numbers, 39
    parallel lines, 91, 284
    rays, 89, 287

right angles, 90
right triangles, 97, 288
subtraction, 48
temperatures below zero, 4, 11
triangles, 96
Novemdecillions, 41
Number facts, 38, 44
Number grids
    definition of, 6–7, 283
    for exploring number patterns,
        6–9
    negative numbers on, 40
    to find differences, 8
Number lines
    decimals on, 12
    definition of, 283
    fractions on, 10, 12, 25–26
    points on, 10, 26
    positive-negative numbers on,
        10, 39–40
    showing gains and losses on, 40
Number models of problems,
    65–68, 186, 190, 283
Number of words children know
    data, 262
Number pairs, 3, 162, 275, 284
Number patterns, 174–175
Number problems, 16, 182
Number stories
    change-to-more, 186
    change-to-less, 186
    comparison, 190
    equal-sharing, 277
    parts-and-total, 188, 284
    solving strategies for, 182
Number uses, 2–5
Numbers
    adjusting, 169–170
    comparisons with, 4, 13, 20,
        26, 36
    composite, 37
    counting, 2, 22–24
    decimal, 3, 33–36, 276
    equal, 13
    even, 9, 38, 174, 278
    fraction, 3, 22–32
    history of, 18
    in codes, 4

    in measurement, 2, 25
    modeling problems with, 283
    negative, 4, 10, 11, 39
    odd, 9, 38, 174, 283
    on number grids, 7
    positive, 10, 39, 285
    prime, 37, 175
    rectangular, 175
    rounding, 170, 288
    square, 175
    to show locations, 3
    triangular, 174
    writing very large and very
        small, 41
Numerator, 11, 22, 31–32, 283

O

Octagon, 95
Octahedron, 104
Odd numbers, 9, 38, 174, 283
Operation symbols
    addition, 48
    division, 67
    multiplication, 65
    subtraction, 48
Ordered pairs of numbers
    for locations on Earth's surface, 3
    for naming coordinates on a
        grid, 162, 275, 284
Ounces, 144

P

Parallel, 284
Parallel lines/segments, 91, 284
Parallelograms, 98–99, 284
Parentheses
    for points on coordinate grids,
        162
    in order of operations, 16–17
Part, 188
Partial-products method of
    multiplication, 58–59, 284
Partial-sums method of addition,
    51–52, 284
Parts-and-total
    diagram, 188
    number story, 188, 284

Patterns
    definition of, 284
    dot picture, 174
    for leap years, 158
    in number grids, 7
    in number stories, 189
    number, 9, 174–175
    picture, 172–173
Pentagon, 95, 275
Pentagonal prism, 106
Per, units in groups, 66, 68, 285
Perimeter
    definition of, 132, 137, 285
    of circles, 134
    of polygons, 132
Personal references, 123, 130
Physical fitness standards, 254–255
Picture patterns, 172–173
Pints, 142
Place, 18–19, 35
Place value
    charts, 19, 20, 35, 36
    definition of, 18, 285
    for counting numbers, 18–19
    games for, 226–229
    history of, 18
    mats, 226–229
    with decimals, 35–36
P.M., 156, 285
Points, 88, 92, 285
Polygons
    definition of, 94, 285
    naming of, 95–96
    sides of, 94
    types of, 94–99
    vertices of, 94
Polyhedrons, 104, 285
Positive numbers
    definition of, 39, 285
    on a number line, 10, 39
Pounds, 144
Precision, 146
Prefixes for polygons, 95–96, 98
Prime numbers, 37–38, 175, 286
Prisms
    congruent, 275
    definition of, 286
    hexagonal, 104, 106

naming, 106
pentagonal, 106
rectangular, 104, 106
triangular, 104, 106, 286
Probability, 85–86, 286
Product, 37, 49
Pyramids
    apex of, 286
    bases of, 105
    definition of, 286
    faces of, 105
    hexagonal, 104–105, 286
    pentagonal, 104–105
    rectangular, 104
    square, 105
    triangular, 104–105
    vertex of, 286

Q

Quadrangles, 95, 98–99, 287
Quadrilaterals, 95, 98, 287
Quantity, 190
Quarts, 142
Quintillions, 41
Quintoquadagintillions, 41

R

Radius, 287, 289
Rainfall in the U.S. data, 245
Range, 73, 287
Rays, 89–90, 92, 287
Rectangles, 63, 99, 288
Rectangular arrays, 63, 175
Rectangular numbers, 175
Rectangular prisms, 106, 140
Regular polygons, 95
Regular polyhedrons, 104
Remainders, 67, 174, 288
Rhombus, 99, 288
Right angle, 90, 288
Right triangle, 97, 288
Rounding numbers, 170, 288
Rows
    in arrays, 58, 63, 66, 272
    in calendars, 6
    in number grids, 6
    in tables and charts, 44

Rule boxes, 176
Rulers
    as number lines, 11
    centimeter scale on, 119
    equivalent fractions on, 28
    fractions on, 25
    inch scale on, 119, 125
Rules, 176, 178

S

Scale, 164
Scale drawings, 164, 288
Scales, for measuring weight, 25,
    146–148
Seasons, 160
Seconds, 156
Septillions, 41
Sextillions, 41
Shapes, 88
Shares, 67, 277
Shipping data for packages, 246–247
Shortcuts
    for area, 138
    for computation, 50
    for equivalent fractions, 29
    for volume of rectangular
        prisms, 141
    turn-around for addition and
        multiplication, 50
Sides, 90, 94, 289
Solid geometry, 102–108
Solids, geometric, 102–108
Spheres
    center of, 108, 273, 289
    definition of, 108, 289
    diameter of, 108, 276
    diagram of, 276, 289
    Earth as a, 108
    radius of, 287, 289
Spinners, 26, 86, 231
Sport balls data, 252–253
Square numbers, 175, 289
Square pyramid, 105
Square units, 136
Standard units of measurement,
    114, 116, 142, 144, 289
Stationery store poster, 238
Stock-up sale posters, 240–241

Subtraction
    counting-up method, 57
    fact triangles, 48
    facts table, 44–45
    games for, 215, 232
    left-to-right method, 56
    on calculators, 215, 217
    trade-first method, 54–55
    using fact triangles, 48
    with a number grid, 8
Surface, 102
Symbols
    for angles, 90
    for comparing numbers, 13, 31
    for degrees, 149
    for line segments, 88
    for lines, 89
    for parallel lines and segments, 91
    for rays, 89
    for right angles, 90
    used with numbers, 5
Symmetry about a line, 111–112

T

Tables
    addition/subtraction facts, 44
    body parts measures, 271
    equivalent fractions, 30
    length of days, 161
    metric system, 122–123, 142,
        144, 270
    months of the year, 158
    multiplication/division facts, 46
    numbers 1 to 20 facts, 38
    seasons of the year, 160
    systems equivalents, 271
    time, 271
    U.S. customary system, 128,
        130, 144, 270
Tallies, 68, 70–71, 283
Tally charts, 70–71, 75, 81, 289
Tally marks, 14, 71, 289
Temperatures
    below zero, 4, 11, 39
    definition of, 289
    finding differences between, 154
    in a change diagram, 187
    in the U.S. in springtime, 244

three hundred seven

on a line graph, 82
on a thermometer, 3, 4, 11, 39
on a weather map, 166
record highs-lows data, 256
Tenths, 33
Tetrahedron, 104
Thermometers, 3, 11, 39, 152–153
Thousandths, 34
Three-dimensional objects, 102,
    108, 139, 290
Thumb measure, 114
Time, 156, 271
Timetables for railroads/airlines, 267
Ton, 144
Tornadoes, 257
Trade-first method of subtraction,
    54–55, 290
Trapezoids, 99, 290
Triangles
    angles of, 96
    definition of, 96, 290
    naming of, 96
    parts of, 96
    prefix for, 96
    sides of, 96
    vertices of, 96
Triangular numbers, 174
Triangular prism, 106
Triangular pyramid, 105
Trillion, 42
Turn-around facts, 50, 290
Two-dimensional figures, 100, 102,
    290

U

Units, 5, 25
Units of Measurement
    based on the human body, 114
    for area, 270
    for capacity, 270
    for length, 116–117, 122,
        128–129
    for time, 156
    for volume, 270
    for weight, 144
    history of, 114
    in the metric system, 114,
        116–123, 142

in the U.S. customary system,
    116–117, 125, 128, 130, 142
U.S. cities population data, 250–251
U.S. customary system, 116–117,
    125, 142, 152, 290
U.S. mileage map, 248–249
U.S. presidents' ages, 266

V

Value, 19, 35, 74
Variety store poster, 239
Vending machine posters, 236–237
Vertex
    definition of, 90, 94, 96, 103,
        291
    of angles, 93
    of geometric solids, 103
    of polygons, 94
    of pyramids, 286
    points, 96, 103
Vertices, 94, 96
Volume
    capacity of containers, 142
    definition of, 291
    measuring with cubes, 139
    units for measuring, 270

W

Weight
    abbreviations for units, 144, 270
    comparisons with different
        units, 145
    definition of, 291
    units for measuring, 144, 270
Weights on the moon, 265
"What's My Rule?", 179, 180
World population growth, 258

Y

Yards, 114, 116, 123, 128, 130
Yardsticks, 119
Years, 156, 158, 160

Z

Zero, 276
Zero mark on a ruler, 11, 120, 126
Zero point on a number line, 10, 39